NEURONALE LERNREGELN UND ANDERE METHODEN FÜR LINEARE ASSOZIATION UND TRENNUNG

Christos Karakas

DIPLOMARBEIT

ISBN 3-89811-233-0
Herstellung: Libri Books on Demand

Inhaltsverzeichnis

Hiermit erkläre ich, daß ich die vorliegende Arbeit selbständig verfaßt und alle benutzten Quellen und Hilfsmittel angegeben habe.

Kaiserslautern, den 13.01.92

Kapitel 1

Einleitung

Der Begriff des neuronalen Netzes hat sich aus den Bemühungen herauskristallisiert, die Funktionsweise des menschlichen Gehirns zu simulieren (s. [6], [63]). Das Bedürfnis einer solchen Simulation entwickelte sich seinerseits Ende der 70er Jahre, als die üblichen, sequentiellen Algorithmen der Künstlichen Intelligenz (KI) ihren Grenzen bei der Realisierung von Funktionen näherten, die das menschliche Gehirn schnell und effektiv durchführt, wie z.b. 'Sehen', 'Sprachverstehen' etc. Zwar existieren die wesentlichen Ansätze, von denen in der Theorie der neuronalen Netze Gebrauch gemacht wird, schon seit den 50er Jahren ([49], [24]), doch mußte es zuerst zur erwähnten Erschöpfung anderer Lösungsansätze kommen, bevor das Interesse der Forscher für dieses Gebiet wieder geweckt wurde. Eine kurze geschichtliche Darstellung findet man in *Richter* [62].

Als Motivation für die nachfolgende formale Behandlung der neuronalen Netzen werden in diesem Abschnitt einige Begriffe aus der Biologie — bewußt schematisch und vereinfacht — dargestellt: (s. [62], [64])

Ein *Neuron*, oder Nervenzelle ist eine Zelle, die elektrische Impulse aussenden und empfangen kann. Die Bestandteile einer solchen Zelle sind:

- Der *Zellkörper* oder *Soma* enthält den Zellkern.

- Der *Axon* ist ein langer Zylinder, der Impulse vom Soma zu anderen Zellen überträgt. Die Vernetzung der Neuronen miteinander erfolgt durch Aufspaltung der Axonen.

- Die *Dendriten* sind kleine Eingangsleitungen zum Neuron.

Eine Kupplungsstelle zwischen zwei Neuronen heißt *Synapse*. Elektrische Signale, die die Synapsen erreichen, haben Signale in den Dendriten zur Folge. Am häufigsten sind Synapsen zwischen Axonen (Sender) und Dendriten (Empfänger).

Folgende Beobachtungen und Annahmen haben den Begriff des neuronalen Netzes entscheidend beinflußt:

- Jedes Neuron kann nur einfache Funktionen erfüllen, doch die Gesamtheit der Neuronen ist zur Durchführung komplizierter Denkvorgänge fähig.

- Die Stärke der Neuronen liegt folglich auf deren Vernetzung.

3

- Man könnte also postulieren, daß die eigentliche Informationsverarbeitung auf den Verbindungen stattfindet und nicht in den Neuronen selbst.

- Neuronen senden gemäß ihres Zustandes Signale aus und diese erreichen je nach Art der Verbindungen andere Neuronen ; dabei werden auch die Verbindungen selbst verändert.

- Die Vorschrift, nach welcher ein Neuron Signale sendet, ist vielleicht eine einfache Funktion (dies hat zum Begriff der *Lernregel* s. Kap. 3) geführt.

Man geht also von der Idee eines neuronalen Netzes aus, das sich aus vielen miteinander verbundenen Neuronen zusammensetzt. Jedes Neuron empfängt Signale von seinen Eingangsneuronen und sendet Signale zu seinen Ausgangsneuronen nach einer noch zu bestimmender Vorschrift. Dieser Gedanke wird im nächsten Kapitel formalisiert. Für eine detailliertere Einführung s. [45], [54], [34], [42] und für eine Übersicht s. [25], [66].

In dieser Arbeit werden einige Algorithmen ('Lernregeln') für neuronale Netze dargestellt und getestet. Im Kapitel 2 werden die Begriffe 'Neuron', 'neuronales Netz' und die damit verbundene Aufgabe der 'linearen Assoziation' mathematisch definiert. Im Kapitel 3 werden Methoden zur Lösung dieser Aufgabe dargestellt. Nicht lineare neuronale Netze, Perceptrons, nicht lineare Assoziation und lineare Trennung werden im Kapitel 4 eingeführt. Im Kapitel 5 werden die Methoden zur Lösung des linearen Trennungsproblems dargestellt und teilweise hinsichtlich ihres theoretischen Verhaltens untersucht. Nicht nur neuronale Lernregeln, sondern auch andere Methoden sind beschrieben. Im letzten Kapitel werden die Ergebnisse einer Computer-Simulation präsentiert. Die Methoden vom Kapitel 5 wurden dabei bezüglich ihrer zeitlichen Effizienz miteinander verglichen.

Mein Dank gilt Herrn Prof. Dr. Prätzel-Wolters für das interessante Thema und die geduldige Betreuung der Arbeit, sowie den Bibliotheken und dem Rechenzentrum der Universität Kaiserslautern, deren Unterstützung diese Arbeit erst möglich machte.

Kapitel 2

Neuronen und neuronale Netze

Die folgenden Definitionen präzisieren die in der Einleitung dargestellten Ansätze bzw. legen den mathematischen Rahmen fest, worin die in dieser Arbeit vorgenommene Behandlung neuronaler Netze stattfinden wird.

Definition 2.1 *Ein Neuron N ist eine Kollektion*

$$\{T, U, \mathcal{U}, \Phi, \mathcal{H}, \varphi(\cdot), \eta(\cdot)\},$$

wobei

1. $T = \mathrm{R}$ *oder* $T = \mathrm{N}$. T *ist die sog. Zeitmenge*

2. $U \subseteq \mathrm{R}$, $\quad \Phi \subseteq \mathrm{R}$, $\quad, \mathcal{H} \subseteq \mathrm{R}$. U *heißt gelegentlich Kontrollbereich,* Φ *heißt auch Zustandsraum und* $\mathcal{H}$ *heißt Ausgangsmenge.*

3. $\mathcal{U}$ *ist die Menge der Eingangsfunktionen. Dies sind Funktionen mit Definitionsbereich* T *und Werten in der Menge* U:

$$\mathcal{U} = \{u \backslash u : T \longrightarrow U\}$$

4. $\varphi(\cdot)$ *ist die sog. Zustandsüberführungsfunktion:*

$$\varphi : \{(t, t', \psi, u(\cdot)) / t, t' \in T, t > t', \psi \in \Phi, u(\cdot) \in \mathcal{U}\} \longrightarrow \Phi$$

Von der Zustandsüberführungsfunktion wird folgendes gefordert:

(a) $\varphi(t, t, \psi, u(\cdot)) = \psi$ *identisch in* $t, \psi, u(\cdot)$ *(Konsistenz)*

(b) $\varphi(t_1, t_0, \psi, u(\cdot)) = \varphi(t_1, t_0, \psi, u'(\cdot)) \forall t_1 > t_0$ *wenn* $u(t) = u'(t)$ *für alle* t *mit* $t_0 \leq t < t_1$ *(Kasualität)*

(c) $\varphi(t_2, t_1, \varphi(t_1, t_0, \psi, u(\cdot)), u(\cdot)) = \varphi(t_2, t_0, \psi, u(\cdot)) \forall t_0, t_1, t_2 \in T$ *mit* $t_0 \leq t_1 \leq t_2$, $\forall \psi \in \Phi$, $\quad \forall u(\cdot) \in \mathcal{U}$ *(Halbgruppeneigenschaft).*

5. $\eta(\cdot)$ *ist die sog. Ausgangsfunktion:*

$$\eta : \{(t, \psi, v) / t \in T, \psi \in \Phi, v \in U\} \longrightarrow \mathcal{H}$$

$\square$

Die obige Definition eines Neurons lehnt sich stark an der Definition eines Kontrollsystems, wie sie in der Kontrolltheorie üblich ist (s. *Knobloch & Kwakernaak* [37] S. 11).

Definition 2.2 *Ein neuronales Netz NN ist eine Kollektion von Neuronen*

$$\{N_1, N_2, \ldots, N_r\}, r \geq 3$$

für welche es eine Unterkollektion

$$\{N_{j_1}, N_{j_2}, \ldots, N_{j_s}\}$$

und eine dazugehörige Kollektion von Indexmengen

$$\{I_{j_1}, I_{j_2}, \ldots, I_{j_s}\}$$

mit

$$r \geq s \geq 1$$
$$j_p \notin \{1, \ldots, r - s\} \qquad \forall p = 1, \ldots, s$$

so daß

$$u_{j_p} : T \longrightarrow U : u_{j_p}(t) = \sum_{k \in I_{j_p}} w_{j_p k} \eta_k(t, \varphi_k(t), u_k(t)) \quad \forall p = 1, \ldots, s$$

Dabei sind

u_{j_p} : *Die Eingangsfunktion des Neurons* N_{j_p}

u_k : *Die Eingangsfunktion des Neurons* N_k.

$\varphi_k(t)$: *Der Zustand des Neurons* N_k *zur Zeit t. Hier wird angenommen, daß für jedes Neuron* N_k *ein* t'_k *und ein* ψ *gegeben sind, so daß* φ_k *als Funktion von t angesehen werden kann, die der Einfachheit halber mit dem selben Symbol angedeutet wird:*

$$\varphi_k(t, t'_k, \psi, u_k(\cdot)) = \varphi_k(t)$$

η_k : *Die Ausgangsfunktion des Neurons* N_k . *Sie kann auch als Funktion von t angesehen werden (s. oben).*

$w_{j_p k}$: *Eine reele Zahl, die oft 'das Gewicht der Verbindung vom Neuron* N_k *zum Neuron* N_{j_p} *genannt wird. Die Matrix* $W := [w_{ik}]$ *mit*

$$w_{ik} = \begin{cases} w_{j_p k} & : \quad i = j_p \in \{j_1, \ldots, j_s\} \quad und \quad k \in I_i \\ 0 & : \quad sonst \end{cases}$$

heißt die Gewichtsmatrix *des Netzes.*

Die Neuronen $N_1, N_2, \ldots, N_{r-s}$ eines neuronalen Netzes NN heißen Eingangsneuronen. *Der Vektor $u(t) = (u_1(t), \ldots, u_{r-s}(t))^\top \in \mathbb{R}^{r-s}$ heißt* Eingangsvektor *des neuronalen Netzes NN. Der Vektor $\varphi(t) = (\varphi_1(t), \ldots, \varphi_r(t))^\top \in \mathbb{R}^r$ heißt* Zustandsvektor *des neuronalen Netzes NN.*

Ferner gibt es für jedes neuronale Netz NN eine Unterkollektion von Neuronen

$$\{N_{q_1}, \ldots, N_{q_m}\}, \quad m \geq 1$$

Die Neuronen N_{q_i}, $i = 1, \ldots, m$ heißen Ausgangsneuronen *und der Vektor $\eta(t) = (\eta_{q_1}(t), \ldots, \eta_{q_m}(t))^\top \in \mathbb{R}^m$* Ausgangsvektor *des neuronalen Netzes NN.*

$\square$

Meistens umfaßt die Menge $\{N_{j_1}, \ldots, N_{j_s}\}$ in der obigen Definition alle Neuronen, die keine Eingangsneuronen sind: $\{N_{j_1}, \ldots, N_{j_s}\} = \{N_{r-s+1}, N_{r-s+2}, \ldots, N_r\}$. Im folgenden wird diese Anordnung angenommen.

Die obige Definition eines neuronalen Netzes ist allgemein genug, um die verschiedenen in der Literatur behandelten neuronalen Netze (s. z.B. *Hopfield* [29,30], *Grossberg* [21,22,23], *Amari* [3,4]) zu umfassen. Je nach Konzeption eignen sich diese Entwürfe für verschiedene Aufgaben z.B. Speicherung und Wiedergabe von Bit-Mustern ([39]), Lösung von Optimierungsproblemen ([31]), oder Kontrollproblemen ([7], [80]), Computer-Sehen ([23]), oder Mustererkennung und -Klassifizierung ([40], [42]). Die in dieser Arbeit untersuchten neuronalen Netze dienen der letzteren Aufgabe.

Die Mustererkennung hat verschiedene Teilaufgaben und mögliche Variationen. Die Aufgabe ist stets so, daß ein Muster vorgelegt wird und 'erkannt' werden soll. Dies kann zweierlei bedeuten (s. *Richter* [62] S. 74):

1. Das Muster soll klassifiziert werden, d.h. ein Klassenindex ist die Ausgabe.

2. Das Muster soll einem anderen zugeordnet werden, d.h. ein weiteres Muster ist die Ausgabe.

Üblicherweise liegen die Muster in Form von Meßwert-Sammlungen vor. Es wird angenommen, daß eine Meßwert-Sammlung die wichtigsten Merkmale eines Musters erfaßt, so daß zwischen dem Muster und seinen Merkmalen — in der Form von Meßwerten — nicht unterschieden wird. Diese Arbeit befaßt sich nicht mit dem Problem einer adäquaten Wahl von Merkmalen eines gegebenen Musters (man siehe in der KI-Literatur unter dem Stichwort 'feature extraction' weiter), sondern nimmt die Merkmal-Vektoren als gegeben an.

Zur Lösung des Problems 2) mittels neuronaler Netzen, benötigt man solche, die Abbildungen zwischen zwei Vektorenmengen herstellen können ([55,56]). Die einfachsten Netze dieser Art sind solche, die lineare Abbildungen implementieren:

Definition 2.3 *Ein* lineares neuronales Netz *LNN ist ein neuronales Netz NN*

$$\{N_1, \ldots, N_l, N_{l+1}, \ldots, N_r\}, \quad r \geq 3, \quad l \geq 1$$

für welches folgendes gilt:

(i) Die Menge der Eingangsneuronen ist

$$\{N_1, \ldots, N_l\} \quad (d.h. \; l = r - s)$$

(ii) Die Menge der Ausgangsneuronen ist

$$\{N_{l+1}, \ldots, N_r\} \quad (d.h. \; m = r - l)$$

(iii) Für jedes $j = 1, \ldots, r$ gilt

$$\varphi_j(t, t', \psi, u(\cdot)) = u_j(t), \quad \forall t, t' \in T, \psi \in \Phi, u(\cdot) \in \mathcal{U}$$

$$\eta_j(t, \psi, u) = u_j(t), \quad \forall t \in T, \psi \in \Phi, u \in U$$

(iv) $U = \Phi = \mathcal{H} = \mathrm{R}$

(v) Für jedes Neuron N_{j_p}, welches nicht Eingangsneuron ist, ist die Menge I_{j_p}, die in Def. 2.2 vorkommt, mit $\{1, \ldots, l\}$ identisch.

$\square$

LNN ist ein neuronales Netz mit zwei Schichten von Neuronen: Eine Eingangsschicht (Neuronen N_1 bis N_l) und eine Ausgangsschicht (Neuronen N_{l+1} bis N_r). Im LNN spielt weder der Zustandsvektor, noch die Vorgeschichte des Eingangs eine Rolle. Für jedes Neuron eines LNN sind Eingang, Zustand und Ausgang gleich. Für sich genommen arbeitet somit jedes Neuron im LNN eher trivial. Die eigentliche Informationsverarbeitung im LNN geschieht lediglich durch die spezielle Struktur des Netzes, verliehen durch (i),(ii) und (v) der Def. 2.3. Wie folgender Satz besagt, implementiert ein LNN eine lineare Eingangs-Ausgangsrelation:

Satz 2.1 *Gegeben sei ein lineares neuronales Netz LNN. Sei $u(t) = (u_1(t), \ldots, u_l(t))^\top$ der Eingangsvektor und $\eta(t) = (\eta_{l+1}(t), \ldots, \eta_r(t))^\top$ der Ausgangsvektor des Netzes. Dann gilt*

$$\eta(t) = W u(t) \quad \forall t \in \mathrm{T} \tag{2.1}$$

mit $W \in \mathrm{R}^{(r-l) \times l} \equiv \mathrm{R}^{m \times l}$ eine Matrix, deren Element an der (i,j)-ten Stelle das Gewicht $w_{(l+i),j}$ ist.

$\square$

Beweis: Folgt leicht aus Def. 2.1, 2.2 und 2.3.

$\square$

Da ein LNN nach obigem Satz den Vektor η zum Vektor u (durch (2.1) assoziiert), kann als sog. 'assoziativer Speicher' (s. [5], [40], [57]) eingesetzt werden. Ein linearer assoziativer Speicher und somit auch ein LNN hat folgendes Problem zu lösen:

Problem 2.1 (Lineare Assoziation) *Gegeben seien zwei Vektorenmengen* $\{u^j\}_{j=1}^p$ *und* $\{\eta^j\}_{j=1}^p$ *mit* $u^j \in \mathrm{R}^l$ *und* $\eta^j \in \mathrm{R}^m$. *Finde eine Matrix* $W \in \mathrm{R}^{m \times l}$, *die folgendes Funktional minimiert:*

$$E : \mathrm{R}^{m \times l} \longrightarrow \mathrm{R}_0^+ : E(W) := \sum_{j=1}^p E^j(W)$$

mit[1]

$$E^j : \mathrm{R}^{m \times l} \longrightarrow \mathrm{R}_0^+ : E^j(W) := \|Wu^j - \eta^j\|_2^2$$

$\square$

Das LNN soll also möglichst gut 'lernen', als Ausgangsvektor $\eta(t^j) = (\eta_1(t^j), \ldots, \eta_m(t^j))^\top$ den gegebenen Vektor η^j zu produzieren, falls zum Zeitpunkt t^j der Eingangsvektor $u(t^j) = (u_1(t^j), \ldots, u_l(t^j))^\top$ gleich dem gegebenen Vektor u^j ist, für alle $j = 1, \ldots, p$. Dies soll mit Hilfe einer Matrix W geschehen, deren Einträge nach Satz 2.1 die Gewichte der Neuronenverbindungen sind (die Idee, eine Matrix für Lernprozesse einzusetzen, erscheint zum ersten Mal in *Steinbuch* [72,73]). Es gilt also, Algorithmen zu bestimmen, die die Gewichte so modifizieren, daß am Ende die gewünschte Matrix entsteht. Solche Algorithmen sind meistens iterativ. Oft nennt man die Iterationsphase auch 'Lernphase'. Nach erfolgreichem Abschluß der Lernphase sagt man, daß das LNN die gewünschte Abbildung 'gelernt' hat. Man kann dann, bei nun fester Gewichtsmatrix W, sein Verhalten bei anderen Eingangsvektoren, als die u^j, untersuchen. Dies nennt man die 'Laufphase' des Netzes. Man beachte, daß hier die Struktur und die Parameter des Netzes als gegeben gelten. In der Praxis muß man nicht nur den Lernalgorithmus, sondern auch die optimale Architektur des Netzes für die gegebene Aufgabe bestimmen. Um Loutrell in *Sutherland et al* [76] zu wiederholen, 'das ist kein Picknick' (s. dazu *Baum* [8,9], *Blum & Rivest* [12], *Judd* [33], *Lin & Vitter* [44]).

---

[1]Für $x \in \mathrm{R}^m$ bezeichnet $\|x\|_p$ die p-Norm von x: $\|x\|_p = (\sum_{i=1}^m |x_i|^p)^{1/p}$.

Kapitel 3

Methoden zur Lösung des linearen Assoziationsproblems

Die Algorithmen zur Lösung des linearen Assoziationsproblems 2.1 für LNN , aber auch andere Algorithmen für neuronale Netze sind iterativ. Da Lernen beim Mensch und Tier oft durch Versuch und Irrtum, oder durch Wiederholung (s. [18]), also iterativ, vor sich geht, spricht man auch von 'Lernalgorithmen' oder 'Lernregeln'. In der folgenden Definition wird zwischen Algorithmus und seinem Produkt — einer Folge von Matrizen — nicht unterschieden.

Definition 3.1 *Eine Lernregel ist eine konvergierende Folge von Gewichtsmatrizen W_n eines neuronalen Netzes NN.*

□

Im folgenden werden einige Lernregel für LNN näher untersucht.

3.1 Die Hebb'sche Lernregel

Die einfachste Lernregel für LNN ist die sog. *Hebb'sche Lernregel.* Sie liefert allerdings nur dann exakte Resultate, falls die Eingangsvektoren u^j gegenseitig orthogonal sind:

Definition 3.2 *Für die Vektorenmenge $\{u^j\}_{j=1}^p, \quad u^j \in \mathrm{R}^l$ gelte:*

$$u^{i^\top} u^j = \begin{cases} \neq 0 & : \quad i = j \\ 0 & : \quad sonst \end{cases}$$

Die Hebb'sche Lernregel wird durch folgende Matrizenfolge definiert:

$$W_n = \begin{cases} \sum_{j=1}^n \dfrac{\eta^j u^{j^\top}}{\|u^j\|_2^2}, & : \quad n = 1, \ldots, p \\ W_{n-1} & : \quad n = p+1, \ldots \end{cases}$$

Hier sind η^j wie in Problem 2.1.

□

10

Setzt man $\Delta W_n = W_n - W_{n-1}$ erhält man für die Hebb'sche Regel

$$\Delta W_n = \frac{\eta^n u^{n\top}}{\|u^n\|_2^2}, \quad n = 2, \ldots, p$$

Für die Einträge der Matrix ΔW_n gilt

$$(\Delta W_n)_{ij} = w_{ij}^n - w_{ij}^{n-1} = \frac{\eta_i^n u_j^n}{\|u^n\|_2^2}, \quad n = 2, \ldots, p$$

wobei η_i^n, u_j^n die i-te bzw. j-te Komponente von η^n bzw. u^n ist. Dies bedeutet, daß die Gewichtsänderung für das Gewicht der Verbindung $N_j \longrightarrow N_i$ proportional zum Produkt von Signal u_j^n des Neurons N_j zum Neuron N_i und gewünschtem Ausgangssignal η_i^n des Neurons N_i ist. Diese einfache Regel, allerdings nicht mathematisch formuliert, geht auf *Hebb* [24] zurück.

Für die Hebb'sche Regel gilt folgender

Satz 3.1 *Für die Eingangsvektoren des linearen Assoziationsproblems 2.1 gelte*

$$u^{i\top} u^j = \begin{cases} \neq 0 & : \quad i = j \\ 0 & : \quad sonst \end{cases}$$

Sei

$$W = \sum_{j=1}^p \frac{\eta^j u^{j\top}}{\|u^j\|_2^2}$$

Dann gilt

$$W u^i = \eta^i, \quad \forall i = 1, \ldots, p$$

$\square$

Beweis :

$$W u^k = \left(\sum_{j=1}^p \frac{\eta^j u^{j\top}}{\|u^j\|_2^2} \right) u^k = \sum_{j=1}^p \frac{\eta^j (u^{j\top} u^k)}{\|u^j\|_2^2} = \sum_{j=1}^p \eta^j \delta_{jk} = \eta^k, \quad \forall k = 1, \ldots, p$$

wobei die Orthogonalitätseigenschaft der Eingangsvektoren verwendet wurde.

$\square$

In der Praxis werden die Eingangsvektoren, falls sie nicht gegenseitig orthogonal sind, zuerst mit Algorithmen verarbeitet, die ihre gegenseitige Orthogonalität maximieren, s. [39].

3.2 Die Delta-Lernregel

Die Hebb'sche Regel liefert exakte Resultate unter der Annahme, daß die Eingangsvektoren u^j gegenseitig orthogonal sind. Dies ist allerdings meist eine zu große Einschränkung. Die in diesem Abschnitt beschriebene Delta-Regel konvergiert zur richtigen Matrix unter milden Annahmen wenn die Eingangsvektoren linear unabhängig sind (s. *Kohonen* [40], *Stone* [75]).

Definition 3.3 *Eine Delta-Lernregel wird (mit den Bezeichnungen von Problem 2.1) wie folgt definiert:*

$$W_0 = 0$$
$$W_n = W_{n-1} + G_n(\eta^{i_n} - W_{n-1}u^{i_n})u^{i_n^\top}$$

mit $W_n, W_{n-1} \in \mathbb{R}^{m \times l}$, $G_n \in \mathbb{R}^{m \times m}$, $\{i_n\}_{n \in \mathbb{N}}$ eine Indexfolge mit Werten in $\{1, \ldots, p\}$. Dabei soll G_n so gewählt werden, daß $\{W_n\}_{n \in \mathbb{N}}$ konvergent ist.

□

Die Matrix G_n heißt 'gain matrix'. Eine wichtige Wahl ist $G_n = a_n I$. Wenn nicht anders bemerkt, wird im folgenden diese Form für G_n verwendet.

Die intuitive Idee hinter der Delta-Regel ist, daß die Änderung der Gewichtsmatrix W_{n-1} abhängig von der Differenz zwischen Ergebnis und Sollwert sein soll. Es gibt eine interessante Beziehung zwischen dieser 'Fehlerkorrektur-Methode' und der Rescorla-Wagner-Theorie der klassischen Konditionierung. *Rescorla & Wagner* [61] behaupten, daß die Organismen nur dann lernen, wenn die Ereignisse ihre Erwartungen widerlegen: 'Nach einem stimulierenden Komplex werden gewisse Erwartungen bzgl. den Ereignissen geformt. Die durch diesen Komplex und seine Komponenten erzeugten Erwartungen werden nur dann modifiziert, wenn die darauf folgenden Ereignisse und die resultierende Erwartung nicht im Einklang sind' (s. auch [66]).

Für den Fall, daß die Eingangsvektoren gegenseitig orthogonal sind, kann man die Hebb'sche Regel als eine Delta-Regel auffassen:

Satz 3.2 *Falls für die Eingangsvektoren u^j gilt*

$$u^{i^\top} u^j = \begin{cases} \neq 0 & : \quad i = j \\ 0 & : \quad sonst \end{cases}$$

für $i, j \in \{1, \ldots, p\}$ und falls

$$G_n = a_n I$$
$$a_n = \frac{1}{\|u^{i_n}\|_2^2}$$

dann gilt für die Delta-Regel von Def. 3.3

$$W_n = \sum_{j \in Q_n} \frac{\eta^j u^{j^\top}}{\|u^j\|_2^2}$$

wobei

$$Q_n := \{i_q, \quad q = 1, \ldots, n\}$$

□

Bemerkung : Da Q_n die Menge der ersten n Terme der Folge $\{i_q\}_{q \in \mathbb{N}}$ ist, treten in der Summe für W_n nur diejenigen Indizes j auf, die voneinander verschieden sind.

Beweis vom Satz 3.2 : Induktion über n:

$$n = 1 \quad : \quad W_1 = W_0 + a_1(\eta^{i_1} - W_0 u^{i_1}) u^{i_1^\top}$$

Da $W_0 = 0$ und $a_1 = \frac{1}{\|u^{i_1}\|_2^2}$ folgt

$$W_1 = \frac{\eta^{i_1} u^{i_1^\top}}{\|u^{i_1}\|_2^2} = \sum_{j \in Q_1} \frac{\eta^j u^{j^\top}}{\|u^j\|_2^2}$$

mit $Q_1 = \{i_1\}$. Angenommen, der Satz gilt für $n = k$:

$$W_k = \sum_{j \in Q_k} \frac{\eta^j u^{j^\top}}{\|u^j\|_2^2}$$
$$Q_k = \{i_q, \quad q = 1, \ldots, k\}$$

Dann ist für $n = k + 1$:

$$W_{k+1} = W_k + a_{k+1}(\eta^{i_{k+1}} - W_k u^{i_{k+1}}) u^{i_{k+1}^\top}$$

Es gilt nach Induktionsannahme und Orthogonalitätsbedingung:

$$W_k u^{i_{k+1}} = \sum_{j \in Q_k} \frac{\eta^j u^{j^\top} u^{i_{k+1}}}{\|u^j\|_2^2}$$
$$= \begin{cases} \frac{\eta^{i_{k+1}} \|u^{i_{k+1}}\|_2^2}{\|u^{i_{k+1}}\|_2^2} = \eta^{i_{k+1}} & : \quad i_{k+1} \in Q_k \\ 0 & : \quad \text{sonst} \end{cases}$$

Da nach Annahme

$$a_{k+1} = \frac{1}{\|u^{i_{k+1}}\|_2^2}$$

erhält man

$$W_{k+1} = W_k + \frac{(\eta^{i_{k+1}} - \eta^{i_{k+1}}) u^{i_{k+1}^\top}}{\|u^{i_{k+1}}\|_2^2} = W_k, \quad \text{falls} \quad i_{k+1} \in Q_k$$

und

$$W_{k+1} = W_k + \frac{\eta^{i_{k+1}} u^{i_{k+1}^\top}}{\|u^{i_{k+1}}\|_2^2}, \quad \text{falls} \quad i_{k+1} \notin Q_k$$

Dies kann man zusammenfassend schreiben, als

$$W_{k+1} = \sum_{j \in Q_{k+1}} \frac{\eta^j u^{j^\top}}{\|u^j\|_2^2}$$

mit $Q_{k+1} = \{i_q, \quad q = 1, \ldots, k+1\}$

□

Korrolar 3.1 *Falls*

$$u^{i^\top} u^j = \begin{cases} \neq 0 & : \quad i = j \\ 0 & : \quad sonst \end{cases}$$

dann liefert die Wahl

$$G_n = a_n I$$
$$a_n = \frac{1}{\|u^{i_n}\|_2^2}$$

mit

$$i_n = \begin{cases} n & : \quad n = 1, \ldots, p \\ beliebig \ aus \ \{1, \ldots, p\} & : \quad n = p + 1, \ldots \end{cases}$$

eine Delta-Regel, die identisch zur Hebb'schen Regel ist

□

Beweis : Aus der Definition von Q_n und der Wahl von i_n folgt:

$$Q_n = \begin{cases} \{1, \ldots, n\} & : \quad n = 1, \ldots, p \\ \{1, \ldots, p\} & : \quad n = p + 1, \ldots \end{cases}$$

Für die Delta-Regel folgt dann aus Satz 3.2

$$W_n = \begin{cases} \sum_{j=1}^n \frac{\eta^j u^{j^\top}}{\|u^j\|_2^2} & : \quad n = 1, \ldots, p \\ W_{n-1} & : \quad n = p + 1, \ldots \end{cases}$$

und dies ist genau die Hebb'sche Regel.

□

Korrollar 3.1 besagt, daß die Hebb'sche Regel eine spezielle Delta-Regel ist. Die Orthogonalitätsbedingung kann gemildert werden, wenn man anstatt der Hebb'schen eine Delta-Regel wählt, für welche die Folgen $\{a_n\}_{n \in \mathbb{N}}$ und $\{i_n\}_{n \in \mathbb{N}}$ gewißen Beschränkungen unterworfen sind. Da dies zuerst für den Fall dargestellt wird, daß das Netz nur ein Ausgangsneuron hat, folgt eine Definition:

Definition 3.4 *Ein* lineares Element *LINE ist ein lineares neuronales Netz LNN mit nur einem Ausgangsneuron, d.h. $l = r - 1$ mit den Bezeichnungen von Def. 2.3. Ein* adaptives lineares Element *ADALINE ist ein lineares Element LINE, dessen Gewichtsmatrix mit Hilfe einer Delta-Regel bestimmt wird.*

$\square$

Bemerkungen :

1. Die Gewichtsmatrix eines linearen Elementes ist ein Zeilenvektor $w \in \mathrm{R}^{1 \times (r-1)}$, $w = (w_{r1}, \ldots, w_{r(r-1)})$ Für die Vektoren u^i, η^i des Problems 2.1 gilt $u^i \in \mathrm{R}^{r-1}, \eta^i \in \mathrm{R}, \quad i = 1, \ldots, p$. Wenn man also die Gewichtsmatrix mit Hilfe eines Vektors w als $w^\top$ schreibt, läßt sich die Rekursionsformel für eine Delta-Regel wie folgt schreiben:

$$w_n^\top = w_{n-1}^\top + a_n(\eta^{i^n} - w_{n-1}^\top u^{i^n})u^{i^n \top} \tag{3.1}$$

2. Das Entsprechende zur Delta-Regel in einer stochastischen Analyse von neuronalen Netzen ist die sog. *Widrow-Hoff-Regel* [77].

3. Mehr über ADALINEs und ihre Anwendungen findet man in *Widrow et al* [78].

Satz 3.3 *Seien $U = [u^1, \ldots, u^p]$ die $(l \times p)$-Matrix, deren Spalten die Eingangsvektoren sind $(l = r - 1)$, $\eta^\top = (\eta^1, \ldots, \eta^p)$ der Zeilenvektor der Zielwerte η^i eines linearen Assoziationsproblems (s. Problem 2.1) für ein lineares adaptives Element und $\{i_n\}_{n \in \mathrm{N}}$ eine Indexfolge mit Werten in $\{1, \ldots, p\}$. Unter den Bedingungen*

(i) $\delta \leq a_n \leq \dfrac{2}{\|u^n\|_2^2} - \delta$ mit δ eine willkürlich kleine feste Zahl, für welche gilt:

$$0 < \delta < \frac{1}{\max_j \|u^j\|_2^2}$$

(ii) $\forall r \in \{1, \ldots, p\}, \forall q \in \mathrm{N} \quad \exists k \geq q : i_k = r$

(iii) Die Eingangsvektoren $u^j, j = 1, \ldots, p$ sind linear unabhängig.

konvergiert die durch (3.1) definierte Folge zu einem Vektor w_* , für welchen gilt

$$w_*^\top U = \eta^\top$$

Die Konvergenz erfolgt bei beliebigem Startvektor w_0

$\square$

Beweis : Siehe *Kohonen* [40,38].

$\square$

Bemerkung : Bedingung (i) ist eher technisch, wobei Bedingung (ii) garantiert, daß in der Folge $\{u^{i^n}\}_{n \in \mathrm{N}}$ bzw. $\{\eta^{i^n}\}_{n \in \mathrm{N}}$ jedes u^r bzw. η^r mit r aus $\{1, \ldots, p\}$ unendlich oft erscheint.

Korrolar 3.2 *Gegeben sei ein lineares neuronales Netz LNN. Unter den Bedingungen (i),(ii) und (iii) vom Satz 3.3 konvergiert jede Delta-Regel zu einer Lösung W des linearen Assoziationsproblems 2.1 mit*

$$E(W) = 0$$

□

Beweis :   Im Falle eines LNN gilt $\eta^j \in \mathrm{R}^m$. Seien $H = [\eta^1, \ldots, \eta^p]$ die $(m \times p)$-Matrix mit Spalten η^i und $U = [u^1, \ldots, u^p] \in \mathrm{R}^{l \times p}$ wie im Satz 3.3. Aus $E(W) = 0$ folgt

$$w_q^\top U = \eta_q^\top, \quad q = 1, \ldots, m$$

wobei $w_q^\top, \eta_q^\top$ die q-te Zeilen der Matrizen W und H sind. Die Aussage des Korollars folgt leicht, wenn man dabei Satz 3.3 m Mal anwendet.

□

Für eine Übertragung der Delta-Regel auf allgemeinere neuronale Netze s. *Rummelhart et al* [65].

3.3   Lösung mit generalisierten Inversen

Einer der Ziele diese Arbeit ist es, die Zusammenhänge der 'neuronalen' Algorithmen zu anderen klassischeren Methoden zu erleuchten. Dabei wird es sich herausstellen, daß es unter den letzteren ganz erwägenswerte Alternativen gibt. Zu dieser Kategorie gehören die Methoden, die sich auf die Berechnung generalisierter Inversen basieren.

Für die folgenden Darstellungen sei die Matrixnorm $\| \cdot \|$ definiert durch

$$\|A\| = \mathrm{tr} A^\top A$$

Daraus folgt leicht, daß das Problem 2.1 äquivalent ist zu folgendem

Problem 3.1 (Lineare Assoziation, äquivalente Formulierung) *Seien $H = [\eta^1, \ldots, \eta^p] \in \mathrm{R}^{m \times p}$ und $U = [u^1, \ldots, u^p] \in \mathrm{R}^{l \times p}$ mit den Bezeichnungen vom Problem 2.1. Finde eine Matrix $W \in \mathrm{R}^{m \times l}$ für welches gilt:*

$$\|WU - H\| \quad \text{ist minimal}$$

□

Dies ist ein gut studiertes Problem der linearen Algebra. Zu seiner Behandlung braucht man einige Begriffe und Resultate aus der Theorie der generalisierten Inversen einer Matrix (s. [2], [60], [10]):

Satz 3.4 *Die vier Gleichungen*

$$
\begin{array}{lll}
A(1) & AXA & = A \\
A(2) & XAX & = X \\
A(3) & (AX)^{\top} & = AX \\
A(4) & (XA)^{\top} & = XA
\end{array}
$$

haben eine eindeutige Lösung X für jede Matrix A

$\square$

Beweis : Siehe *Penrose* [58].

$\square$

Die Bezeichnung $A\{i, j, \ldots, l\}$ steht für die Menge der Matrizen $X \in \mathbb{R}^{m \times l}$, welche die Gleichungen A(i),A(j),...,A(l) aus den Gleichungen A(1),A(2),A(3),A(4) erfüllen. Eine Matrix $X \in A\{i, j, \ldots, l\}$ heißt eine $\{i, j, \ldots, l\}$-Inverse von A. Zum Beispiel heißt eine Matrix, die A(1) und A(2) erfüllt, eine $\{1, 2\}$-Inverse von A. Die $\{1, 2, 3, 4\}$-Inverse von A heißt die *Moore-Penrose-Inverse* von A und wird mit A^{+} bezeichnet.

Sei $A \in \mathbb{R}^{m \times n}$. Mit R(A), N(A) werden folgende Mengen bezeichnet:

$$
\begin{array}{lll}
R(A) & = & \{y \in \mathbb{R}^{m}/y = Ax \quad \text{für ein} \quad x \in \mathbb{R}^{n}\} \\
N(A) & = & \{x \in \mathbb{R}^{n}/Ax = 0\}
\end{array}
$$

Lemma 3.1 *Für jede Matrix A gilt* $N(A) = R^{\perp}(A^{\top})$.

$\square$

Beweis : Siehe *Albert* [2], Th.2.10.

$\square$

Definition 3.5 *Sei* $S \subset \mathbb{R}^{n}$ *ein Unterraum. Die Matrix* $P \in \mathbb{R}^{n \times n}$ *heißt die* orthogonale Projektion auf S , *falls*

$$
\begin{array}{rll}
R(P) & = & S \hspace{3cm} (3.2) \\
P^{2} & = & P \hspace{3cm} (3.3) \\
P^{\top} & = & P \hspace{3cm} (3.4)
\end{array}
$$

$\square$

Es gilt folgendes

Lemma 3.2 *Jede orthogonale Projektion P ist positiv-semidefinit.*

☐

Beweis : Nach (3.3), (3.4) von Def. 3.5

$$x^\top P x = x^\top P P x = x^\top P^\top P x = \|Px\|_2^2 \geq 0$$

☐

Folgendes Lemma wird später gebraucht:

Lemma 3.3 *Die Matrizen* AA^+, $I - AA^+$ *sind positiv-semidefinit.*

☐

Beweis : Nach Korollar 3.5 in *Albert* [2] ist AA^+ die orthogonale Projektion auf R(A) und $I - AA^+$ die orthogonale Projektion auf N($A^\top$). Die Behauptung folgt somit direkt aus Lemma 3.2.

☐

Definition 3.6 *Seien* X, X_0, G *Matrizen aus* $\mathrm{R}^{m \times l}$ *und* f *eine beliebige Funktion:*

$$f : \mathrm{R}^{m \times l} \longrightarrow \mathrm{R}^{m \times l}$$

X_0 *heißt 'eine beste Näherungslösung der Gleichung* $f(X) = G$ ', *falls für alle* X *entweder*

$$\text{C(1):} \quad \|f(X) - G\| > \|f(X_0) - G\|$$

oder

$$\text{C(2):} \quad \|f(X) - G\| = \|f(X_0) - G\| \quad und \quad \|X\| \geq \|X_0\|$$

gilt.

☐

Satz 3.5 *Seien* A, B, C, X *beliebige reelle Matrizen. Die eindeutige beste Näherungslösung der Gleichung*

$$AXC = B$$

ist $A^+ B C^+$.

☐

Beweis : Siehe *Penrose* [59].

☐

Korrolar 3.3 *Seien* W, U, H *beliebige reelle Matrizen. Die eindeutige beste Näherungslösung der Gleichung*

$$WU = H$$

ist $W = H U^+$.

□

Definition 3.7 *Ein X_0, welches die Bed. C(1) von Def. 3.6 erfüllt, heißt 'eine least-squares-Lösung von $f(X) = G$'. Ein X_0, welches die Bed. C(2) erfüllt, heißt 'eine Minimum-Norm-Lösung von $f(X) = G$'.*

□

In der äquivalenten Formulierung 3.1 vom Problem 2.1 geht es also darum, eine least-squares-Lösung von $WU = H$ zu finden. Der folgende Satz liefert sie:

Satz 3.6 *Die allgemeine least-squares-Lösung der Gleichung*

$$WU = H$$

— und somit die allgemeine Lösung des Problems 2.1 bzw. 3.1 — ist

$$W = HU^{(1,3)} + Z(I - UU^{(1,3)}) \tag{3.5}$$

Dabei sind

$$W \in R^{m \times l}, \quad U \in R^{l \times p}, \quad H \in R^{m \times p}$$

gegeben,

$$Z \in R^{m \times l}, \quad \text{beliebig und}$$
$$U^{(1,3)} \in U\{1, 3\}.$$

□

Beweis : Folgt aus *Ben-Israel & Greville* [10] S. 119, S. 42.

□

Bemerkung : Satz 3.6 besagt, daß die Lösungen vom Problem 2.1 bwz. 3.1 eine Familie, gegeben durch (3.5), bilden. Um eine Lösung zu finden, braucht man eine $\{1,3\}$-Inverse von U zu berechnen. Nur die Minimum-Norm-Lösung ist eindeutig. Obwohl zur Lösung vom Problem 2.1 eine $\{1,3\}$-Inverse genügt, wird im folgenden nur die Moore-Penrose-Inverse betrachtet.

Ein bekannter Algorithmus zur Berechnung der Moore-Penrose-Inverse U^+ ist der Algorithmus von *Greville* (s. *Kohonen* [40] S. 42). Wenn man eine Matrix U mit k Spalten durch U_k bezeichnet und sie als $U_k = [U_{k-1} : u^k]$ teilt, wobei U_{k-1} eine Matrix mit $k - 1$ Spalten ist, dann ermöglicht der Algorithmus von Greville U_k^+ mit Hilfe von U_{k-1}^+ zu berechnen:

Satz 3.7 (Algorithmus von Greville) *Es gilt:*

$$U_k^+ = \left[\begin{array}{c} U_{k-1}^+(I - u^k p_k^\top) \\ p_k^\top \end{array} \right]$$

mit

$$p_k = \begin{cases} \dfrac{(I - U_{k-1}U_{k-1}^+)u^k}{\|(I - U_{k-1}U_{k-1}^+)u^k\|_2^2} & : \quad \textit{Zähler ungleich Null} \\[3mm] \dfrac{U_{k-1}^{+\top}U_{k-1}^+u^k}{1 + \|U_{k-1}^+u^k\|_2^2} & : \quad \textit{sonst} \end{cases}$$

Der Anfangswert U_1 ist gleich der ersten Spalte u^1 von U, wobei dann

$$u_1^+ = \begin{cases} u^{1\top}(u^{1\top}u^1)^{-1} & : \quad u^1 \neq 0 \\ 0 & : \quad u^1 = 0 \end{cases}$$

□

Beweis :   Siehe *Ben-Israel & Greville* [10] S. 219, *Kohonen* [40] S. 43.

□

Für die Matrix H verwendet man die selbe Notation, wie für U:

$$H_k = [H_{k-1} : \eta^k], \quad k = 1, \ldots, p$$

und $H_1 = \eta^1$ (also $H_p = H$). Ziel ist, eine Formel für HU^+ herzuleiten, um nicht zuerst U^+ berechnen zu müssen (*Kohonen* [40] S. 123). Wenn man $H_kU_k^+$ mit W_k bezeichnet, dann gilt:

$$\begin{aligned} W_k = H_kU_k &= [H_{k-1} : \eta^k] \left[\begin{array}{c} U_{k-1}^+(I - u^k p_k^\top) \\ p_k^\top \end{array} \right] = \\ &= H_{k-1}U_{k-1}^+ + (\eta^k - H_{k-1}U_{k-1}^+u^k)p_k^\top \Rightarrow \\ \Rightarrow W_k &= W_{k-1} + (\eta^k - W_{k-1}u^k)p_k^\top, \quad k = 2, \ldots, p \end{aligned} \tag{3.6}$$

Die Rekursion 3.6 hat die selbe Form, wie diejenige einer Delta-Regel, da $p_k = a_k u^k$ für geeignete a_k, die aus dem Satz 3.7 ersichtlich sind.

Der Algorithmus von Greville hat gegenüber der Delta-Regel zwei theoretische Vorteile:

1. Die Eingangsvektore können auch linear abhängig sein.

2. Nach genau p Schritten gelangt man zur Lösung $W = W_p = HU^+$. Somit braucht man die Eingangsvektoren nur einmal dem Netz zu presentieren.

Diese sind, verglichen mit Bed. (ii), (iii) vom Satz 3.3, starke Vorteile vom Algorithmus von Greville, der, destotrotz in der gegenwärtigen Literatur über neuronale Netze eher wenig Beachtung findet.

Kapitel 4

Nicht lineare neuronale Netze

Da das lineare Assoziationsproblem 2.1, 3.1 nicht immer eine Lösung W besitzt, für welche der Fehler $E(W)$ Null ist, hat man versucht, in den neuronalen Netzen Nicht-Linearitäten einzubauen, in der Hoffnung, dadurch eine größere Klasse von Assoziationsproblemen möglichst exakt behandeln zu können. Die in diesem Abschnitt betrachtete nicht-lineare NN sind ausschließlich von folgendem Typ:

Definition 4.1 *Ein nicht-lineares neuronales Netz NLNN ist ein neuronales Netz NN (s. Def. 2.2) für welches gilt, daß für alle Neuronen, die keine Eingangsneuronen sind, die Ausgangsfunktion eine nicht-lineare Funktion des Zustandes des Neurons ist:*

$$\forall j = r - s + 1, \ldots, r \quad : \quad \eta_j(t, \psi, u) = g_j(\varphi_j(t)) \quad g_j \quad nicht\text{-}linear$$

□

Die in der Praxis meist auftretenden Funktionen g_j sind folgende zwei:

1.

$$g_j(x) = \begin{cases} +1 & : \quad x > 0 \\ 0 & : \quad x = 0 \quad \text{(Harte Nicht-Linearität)} \\ -1 & : \quad x < 0 \end{cases}$$

2.

$$g_j(x) = \frac{1}{1 + e^{-x}} \quad \text{Sigmoide}$$

Die in dieser Arbeit behandelten NLNN haben ihre Neuronen in zwei Schichten angeordnet, eine Eingangs- und eine Ausgangsschicht. Die Eingangsschicht wird allerdings nicht zu den eigentlichen Schichten des Netzes gezählt:

Definition 4.2 *Ein nicht-lineares neuronales Netz mit einer Schicht NLNN(1) ist ein nicht-lineares neuronales Netz NLNN — s. Def. 4.1 —, für welches folgende Bedingungen gelten:*

21

(i) Die Bed. *(i)*, *(ii)*, *(iv)*, *(v)* von Def. 2.3

(ii) Für jedes $j = 1, \ldots, r$ gilt

$$\varphi_j(t, t', \psi, u(\cdot)) = u_j(t), \quad \forall t, t' \in T, \psi \in \Phi, u(\cdot) \in \mathcal{U}$$

Für jedes $j = 1, \ldots, r - s$ gilt

$$\eta_j(t, \psi, u) = u_j(t), \quad \forall t \in T, \psi \in \Phi, u \in U$$

Ein nicht-lineares neuronales Netz mit einer Schicht NLNN(1), welches nur ein Ausgangsneuron hat, d.h. für welches $l = r - 1$ gilt, heißt nicht-lineares Element *NLINE.*

□

Bemerkung : Der einzige Unterschied von (ii) oben zu Bed. (iii) von Def. 2.3 liegt in dem teilweise anderen Geltungsbereich für j : $j = 1, \ldots, r - s$ im Gegensatz zu $j = 1, \ldots, r$. Die Menge $\{1, \ldots, r - s\}$ indiziert die Eingangsneuronen.

Eine berühmte Kategorie nicht-linearer neuronaler Netze sind die sog. *Perceptrons* (s. *Rosenblatt* [63], *Minsky & Papert* [51]):

Definition 4.3 *Ein Perceptron ist ein nicht-lineares Element NLINE (s. Def. 4.2), für welches*

$$g_r(x) = \begin{cases} +1 & : \quad x > 0 \\ 0 & : \quad x = 0 \\ -1 & : \quad x < 0 \end{cases}$$

gilt, d.h. die nicht-lineare Ausgangsfunktion des Ausgangsneurons ist eine harte Nicht-Linearität.

□

Für NLNN(1) gilt eine Verallgemeinerung vom Satz 2.1 :

Satz 4.1 *Gegeben sei ein NLNN(1). Sei $u(t) = (u_1(t), \ldots, u_l(t))^\top$ der Eingangsvektor und $\eta(t) = (g_{l+1}(\varphi_{l+1}(t)), \ldots, g_r(\varphi_r(t)))^\top$ der Ausgangsvektor des Netzes. Dann gilt*

$$\eta(t) = g(W u(t))$$

mit $W \in \mathrm{R}^{(r-l) \times l} \equiv \mathrm{R}^{m \times l}$ eine Matrix, deren Element an der (i, j) -ten Stelle das Gewicht $w_{(l+i),j}$ ist und

$$g : \mathrm{R}^m \longrightarrow \mathrm{R}^m : g(x_1, \ldots, x_m) = (g_{l+1}(x_1), \ldots, g_r(x_m))$$

□

Beweis: Folgt leicht aus Def. 2.1, 2.2, 4.1 und 4.2 in der selben Weise, wie für Satz 2.1.

□

Im Einklang zum obigen Satz hat ein NLNN(1) folgendes Problem zu lösen:

Problem 4.1 (Nicht-Lineare Assoziation) *Gegeben seien ein NLNN(1) und zwei Vektorenmengen $\{u^j\}_{j=1}^p$ und $\{\eta^j\}_{j=1}^p$ mit $u^j \in \mathrm{R}^l$ und $\eta^j \in \mathrm{R}^m$. Seien $H = [\eta^1, \ldots, \eta^p] \in \mathrm{R}^{m \times p}$ und $U = [u^1, \ldots, u^p] \in \mathrm{R}^{l \times p}$ Finde eine Matrix $W \in \mathrm{R}^{m \times l}$, die folgendes Funktional minimiert:*

$$E(W) := \|G(WU) - H\|$$

Dabei ist

$$\|A\| = \mathrm{tr}\,AA^\top$$
$$G : \mathrm{R}^{m \times p} \longrightarrow \mathrm{R}^{m \times p} \quad : \quad [a_{ij}] = A \mapsto G(A) = [G(A)_{ij}]$$
$$G(A)_{ij} = g_{i+l}(a_{ij}), \quad i = 1, \ldots, m, \quad j = 1, \ldots, p$$
$$g_{i+l} : \mathrm{R} \to \mathrm{R} \quad : \quad \text{Ausgangsfunktion von } N_{i+l}$$

□

Bemerkung : Mit den obigen Bezeichnungen ist es leicht zu sehen, daß die j-te Spalte der Matrix $G(WU)$ der Vektor $g(Wu^j)$ ist, $j = 1, \ldots, p$ mit g wie im Satz 4.1. Das obige Problem verlangt also nach einer 'möglichst guten' Lösung W der Gleichungen

$$g(Wu^j) = \eta^j, \quad j = 1, \ldots, p.$$

Im Rest dieser Arbeit wird das Problem 4.1 nur im Perceptron-Fall untersucht. Dann gilt $m = 1$, also $\eta^j \in \mathrm{R}$, $\mathrm{R}^{m \times p} \equiv \mathrm{R}^p$, $WU, H \in \mathrm{R}^{1 \times p} \equiv \mathrm{R}^p$, $W \in \mathrm{R}^{m \times l} \equiv \mathrm{R}^l$ und

$$G : \mathrm{R}^p \to \mathrm{R}^p : x = (x_1, \ldots, x_p)^\top \mapsto G(x) = (g_{l+1}(x_1), \ldots, g_{l+1}(x_p))^\top$$

Die Matrixnorm $\|W\|$ ist gleich der Vektornorm $\|W\|_2$ für $W \in \mathrm{R}^{m \times l} \equiv \mathrm{R}^l$. Damit der Fall $E(W) = 0$ nicht vom Anfang an ausgeschlossen bleibt, wird angenommen, daß H im Wertebereich der Funktion G liegt:

$$H \in \{-1, 0, +1\}^p$$

(g_{l+1} ist eine harte Nicht-Linearität). In dieser Arbeit, so wie auch in der Praxis üblich ist, wird sogar

$$H \in \{-1, +1\}^p$$

gelten. Das Problem 4.1 wird dann für die Perceptrons, einen Vektor $w \in \mathrm{R}^l$ zu finden, der folgende Ungleichungen

$$\left\{ \begin{array}{lll} w^\top u^j > 0 & : & \eta^j = +1 \\ w^\top u^j < 0 & : & \eta^j = -1 \end{array} \right\} \tag{4.1}$$

'möglichst gut' löst. Mit den Bezeichnungen

$$U^{(+)} = \{u^j \in \mathbb{R}^l / \eta^j > 0\}$$
$$U^{(-)} = \{u^j \in \mathbb{R}^l / \eta^j < 0\}$$

sind (4.1) äquivalent zu

$$\left\{ \begin{array}{lll} w^\top u > 0 & : & u \in U^{(+)} \\ w^\top u < 0 & : & u \in U^{(-)} \end{array} \right\} \tag{4.2}$$

Das obige Problem für Perceptrons tritt in natürlicher Weise bei der Theorie der Musterklassifikation auf. Dabei geht es darum, verschiedene Musterklassen voneinander mittels geeigneter Funktionen zu unterscheiden. Man geht da im allgemeinen wie folgt vor ([16], [50]):

- Von den Mustern werden geeignete Merkmalvektoren $u^j \in \mathbb{R}^l$ konstruiert. Die Menge $M := \{u^j, \quad j = 1, \ldots, p\}$ gilt hier als gegeben.

- Es werden q disjunkte Klassen $K_i, \quad i = 1, \ldots, q \quad q \geq 2$, von Vektoren gegeben, für welche $M = \cup_{i=1}^q K_i$ gilt.

- Eine Abbildung

$$h : \{1, \ldots, p\} \to \{1, \ldots, q\} : j \mapsto h(j)$$

wird definiert. Dies hat den Sinn, daß der Vektor u^j der Klasse $K_{h(j)}$ zugeordnet werden soll.

- Die Zuordnung geschieht mittels geeigneter *Entscheidungsfunktionen* g_i:

$$g_i : \mathbb{R}^l \to \mathbb{R} : u \mapsto g_i(u), \quad i = 1, \ldots, q$$

die die *Entscheidungsregionen* R_i wie folgt bestimmen:

$$R_i := \{u \in \mathbb{R}^l / g_i(u) > g_n(u), \quad \forall n = 1, \ldots, i-1, i+1, \ldots, q\}$$

- Sei $R(u^j)$ die Entscheidungsregion, die u^j enthält. Dann ist das Problem der Musterklassifikation, geeignete Entscheidungsfunktionen g_i zu finden, so daß

$$K_{h(j)} \subseteq R(u^j), \quad \forall j = 1, \ldots, p$$

Die einfachste Wahl für die g_i's sind affine Funktionen:

$$g_i : \mathbb{R}^l \to \mathbb{R} : u \mapsto g_i(u) = w_i^\top u + w_{i0}, \quad w_i \in \mathbb{R}^l, \quad w_{i0} \in \mathbb{R}$$

O.B.d.A. kann man aber für affine g_i's eine lineare Form annehmen, denn es gilt

$$g_i(u) = w_i'^\top u'$$

mit

$$w_i' = (w_i, w_{i0})^\top \in \mathbb{R}^{l+1}$$
$$u' = (u, 1)^\top \in \mathbb{R}^{l+1}$$

Im folgenden wird immer die lineare Form angenommen.

Das Assoziationsproblem für Perceptrons ist genau das Problem der Musterklassifikation mittels linearer Entscheidungsfunktionen , falls es nur zwei Klassen K_1 und K_2 gibt. (Der Fall von mehreren Klassen kann auf den Zwei-Klassen-Fall reduziert bzw. mit modifizierten Zwei-Klassen-Algorithmen behandelt werden, s. *Sklansky & Wassel* [69] S. 47, *Duda & Hart* [16] S. 174, *Smith* [71], *Mangasarian* [47], *Duda & Fossum* [15], *Meisel* [50] S. 72). Denn sei

$$f : R^l \to R : u \mapsto f(u) := g_1(u) - g_2(u)$$

Dann ist

$$f(u) = w_1^\top u - w_2^\top u = (w_1 - w_2)^\top u = w^\top u$$

mit $w := w_1 - w_2$. Da es zwei Klassen gibt, gilt $h(j) \in \{1, 2\}$ und es gibt nur zwei Entscheidungsregionen R_1 und R_2, gekennzeichnet durch

$$R_1 = \{u \in R^l \quad /w^\top u > 0\}$$
$$R_2 = \{u \in R^l \quad /w^\top u < 0\}$$

Es muß also

$$K_1 \subseteq R_1$$
$$K_2 \subseteq R_2$$

oder

$$K_1 \subseteq R_2$$
$$K_2 \subseteq R_1$$

gelten. Dies ist äquivalent zu

$$w^\top u > 0 \quad \forall u \in K_1$$
$$w^\top u < 0 \quad \forall u \in K_2$$

oder

$$w^\top u > 0 \quad \forall u \in K_2$$
$$w^\top u < 0 \quad \forall u \in K_1,$$

was wiederum genau die Forderung (4.2) mit geeignet gewählten $U^{(+)}$ und $U^{(-)}$ ist. Die Entscheidungsregionen sind die Unterräume, die durch die Hyperebene $w^\top u = 0$ definiert sind. Diese Hyperebene soll also die Mengen K_1 und K_2 bzw. $U^{(+)}$ und $U^{(-)}$ 'trennen'. Für allgemeinere Trennungsflächen siehe *Houle* [32].

Der Begriff der linearen Trennbarkeit gibt es in verschiedenen — mehr oder minder strikten — Auffassungen (s. *Kolmogorov & Fomin* [41] S.129, *Stoer & Witzgall* [74] S. 96). Für Perceptrons ist folgende Definition ausreichend:

Definition 4.4 *Zwei Mengen* $M, N \in \mathbb{R}^n$ *heißen strikt linear trennbar, falls es ein* $w \in \mathbb{R}^n$ *gibt, so daß*

$$w^\top x : \begin{cases} > 0 & : & x \in M \\ < 0 & : & x \in N \end{cases}$$

$\square$

Bemerkung: Man sagt auch, daß w eine 'Dichotomie'[1] der Menge $M \cup N$ definiert. Interessante kombinatorische Eigenschaften von Dichotomien sind in *Cover* [13] zu finden.

Es gelten folgende Sätze:

Satz 4.2 (Kirchberger) *Zwei endlichen Untermengen* M *und* N *von* $\mathbb{R}^n$ *sind strikt linear trennbar, dann und nur dann, wenn für jede Menge* T, *die maximal* $n+2$ *Punkte von* $M \cup N$ *enthält, die Mengen* $T \cap M$ *und* $T \cap N$ *strikt linear trennbar sind.*

$\square$

Beweis : S. *Kirchberger* [36].

$\square$

Satz 4.3 *Zwei abgeschlossene und beschränkte Mengen sind dann und nur dann strikt linear trennbar, wenn ihre konvexe Hüllen leeren Durchschnitt haben.*

$\square$

Beweis : Siehe *Sklansky & Wassel* [69] S. 33-34.

$\square$

Da eine endliche Menge abgeschlossen und beschränkt ist, trifft obiger Satz bei allen endlichen Mengen in dieser Arbeit zu.

Im folgenden werden verschiedene Methoden des linearen Trennungsproblems dargestellt. Dabei werden nicht nur 'neuronale' Algorithmen berücksichtigt, sondern auch klassischere Alternativen.

---

[1]Aus dem griechischen $\delta\iota\chi o\tau o\mu\tilde{\omega}$: in zwei Teile spalten.

Kapitel 5

Methoden zur Lösung des linearen Trennungsproblems

Wenn man

$$U_{(-)} = \{u \in \mathbb{R}^l / -u \in U^{(-)}\}$$
$$F = U^{(+)} \cup U_{(-)}$$

setzt, kann man die Ungleichungen (4.2) wie folgt schreiben:

$$w^\top u > 0 \quad \forall u \in F \tag{5.1}$$

oder auch

$$A^\top w > 0$$

mit $A \in \mathbb{R}^{l \times p}$ eine Matrix, derer Spalten die Vektoren $u \in F$ sind. Dabei bedeutet $x > 0$ für einen Vektor $x \in \mathbb{R}^l$, daß $x_i > 0 \quad \forall i = 1, \ldots, l$ mit x_i die i-te Koordinate von x. Das lineare Trennungsproblem transformiert sich somit in dem Problem, eine Lösung eines Systems linearer Ungleichungen zu finden. Dazu sind in den 60er und 70er Jahren verschiedene Methoden entwickelt. Hinzu kommen ältere Methoden, hauptsächlich Fourier's Eliminierungsmethode ([79], [43], [14], [17]), sowie moderne spiel-theoretische Ansätze ([69], [68]). Fourier's Methode ist rechnerisch unvertretbar und auf Spieltheorie wird im folgenden bewußt nicht eingegangen. Die wichtigsten übrigbleibenden Methoden sind:

5.1 Die Perceptron-Lernregel

Eine der bekanntesten und einfachsten Methoden zur Lösung eines Systems linearer Ungleichungen ist folgender (s. z.B. [51])

Algorithmus 5.1 (Perceptron-Algorithmus) *Gegeben sei eine Matrix $A \in \mathbb{R}^{l \times p}$. Die Vektorfolge $\{w_n \in \mathbb{R}^l\}_{n \in \mathbb{N}}$ definiert durch*

$$w_1 = \quad beliebig$$
$$w_{n+1} = \begin{cases} w_n & : \quad w_n^\top a_j > 0 \quad \forall j \in \{1, \ldots, p\} \\ w_n + a_{i_n} & : \quad \exists i_n \in \{1, \ldots, p\} \quad w_n^\top a_{i_n} \leq 0 \end{cases} \tag{5.2}$$

27

mit a_j die j-te Spalte von A, heißt Perceptron-Algorithmus.

☐

Für den Perceptron-Algorithmus gilt folgender

Satz 5.1 (Perceptron-Konvergenztheorem) *Falls es ein w_* gibt, mit $A^\top w_* > 0$, dann wird $\{w_n\}_{n\in\mathbb{N}}$, definiert durch (5.2) nach endlich vielen Schritten stationär, d.h.*

$$\exists n_0 \in \mathbb{N} : w_n = w_{n_0} \quad \forall n \geq n_0$$

Somit ist w_{n_0} eine Lösung von $A^\top w > 0$.

☐

Beweis : Siehe *Block & Levin* [11], *Minsky & Papert* [51] S. 164-175.

☐

Falls also das System $A^\top w > 0$ lösbar ist, definiert der Perceptron-Algorithmus 5.1 durch (5.2) eine Lernregel im Sinne von Def. 3.1, die *Perceptron-Lernregel*. Falls das System $A^\top w > 0$ unlösbar ist, ist die Folge $\{w_n\}_{n\in\mathbb{N}}$ nicht stationär. Auf jedem Fall bleibt sie jedoch beschränkt, wie folgender Satz versichert:

Satz 5.2 (Perceptron-Beschränktheitstheorem) *Sei $\{w_n\}_{n\in\mathbb{N}}$ definiert durch (5.2). Dann gilt*

$$\|w_n\| \leq \|w_1\| + M \quad ,$$

wobei M eine Konstante ist, die von A, aber nicht von w_1 abhängig ist.

☐

Beweis : Siehe *Block & Levin* [11].

☐

Dem Autor ist weder eine Methode zum effektiven Abbruch im unlösbaren Fall, noch eine Abschätzung der Schranke M bekannt.

Der Perceptron-Algorithmus läßt sich wie folgt verallgemeinern:

$$
\begin{aligned}
w_1 &= \text{beliebig} \\
w_{n+1} &= \left\{
\begin{array}{ll}
w_n & : \; w_n^\top a_j > 0 \quad \forall j \in \{1,\ldots,p\} \\
w_n + \varrho_n a_{i_n} & : \; \exists i_n \in \{1,\ldots,p\} \quad w_n^\top a_{i_n} \leq 0
\end{array}
\right. \\
\varrho_n &> 0 \quad \text{beliebige beschränkte reele Folge mit } \inf_{n\in\mathbb{N}}\{\varrho_n\} > 0
\end{aligned}
\tag{5.3}
$$

Es gilt analog zu Satz 5.1

Satz 5.3 (Verallgemeinertes Perceptron-Konvergenztheorem) *Falls es ein w_* gibt, mit $A^\top w_* > 0$, dann wird $\{w_n\}_{n\in\mathbb{N}}$ definiert durch (5.3) nach endlich vielen Schritten stationär, d.h.*

$$\exists n_0 \in \mathbb{N} : w_n = w_{n_0} \quad \forall n \geq n_0$$

Somit ist w_{n_0} eine Lösung von $A^\top w > 0$

□

Beweis: (Analog zu Satz 5.1 und *Sklansky & Wassel* [69] S.44): Sei w_* eine Lösung von $A^\top w > 0$ Definiere

$$\alpha = \inf_{n\in\mathbb{N}}\{\varrho_n\} \min_{j\in\{1,\ldots,p\}}\{w_*^\top a_j\}$$

$$\beta = \sup_{n\in\mathbb{N}}\{\varrho_n\} \max_{j\in\{1,\ldots,p\}}\{\|a_j\|_2\}$$

$$\overline{w} = \frac{\beta^2}{\alpha}w_* \qquad (5.4)$$

Für den Fall $w_{n+1} \neq w_n$ gilt

$$\|w_{n+1} - \overline{w}\|_2^2 = \|w_n - \overline{w}\|_2^2 + 2(w_n - \overline{w})^\top \varrho_n a_{i_n} + \varrho_n^2\|a_{i_n}\|_2^2 \leq$$
$$\|w_n - \overline{w}\|_2^2 - 2\varrho_n\overline{w}^\top a_{i_n} + \beta^2 \leq \|w_n - \overline{w}\|_2^2 - \beta^2 \qquad (5.5)$$

da $w_n^\top a_{i_n} \leq 0$ und aus (5.4)

$$\frac{\varrho_n w_*^\top a_{i_n}}{\inf_{n\in\mathbb{N}}\{\varrho_n\} \min_{j\in\{1,\ldots,p\}}\{w_*^\top a_j\}} \geq 1 \Rightarrow \varrho_n\frac{\beta^2 w_*^\top a_{i_n}}{\alpha} \geq \beta^2 \Rightarrow \varrho_n\overline{w}^\top a_{i_n} \geq \beta^2 \qquad (5.6)$$

Aus (5.3) folgt, daß falls $w_{n+1} \neq w_n$ ist, dann ist $w_{k+1} \neq w_k$ für $1 \leq k \leq n$. Man darf somit (5.5) n Mal anwenden und es folgt:

$$0 \leq \|w_{n+1} - \overline{w}\|_2^2 \leq \|w_1 - \overline{w}\|_2^2 - n\beta^2$$

Also

$$n \leq \frac{\|w_1 - \overline{w}\|_2^2}{\beta^2}$$

für alle n, für welche ein $i_n \in \{1,\ldots,p\}$ existiert, so daß $w_*^\top a_{i_n} \leq 0$. Man kann also ([·] bezeichnet den Gauß-Klammer)

$$n_0 = \left[\frac{\|w_1 - \overline{w}\|_2^2}{\beta^2}\right] + 1 \qquad (5.7)$$

nehmen und es gilt

$$w_{n_0}^\top a_j > 0 \quad \forall j \in \{1,\ldots,p\}$$

und somit aus (5.3)

$$w_n = w_{n_0} \quad \forall n \geq n_0$$

□

5.2 Die Relaxations-Lernregel

Die in diesem Abschnitt beschriebene Relaxationsmethode kann eingesetzt werden, um eine Lösung eines linearen Ungleichungssystems der Form

$$Aw - b \geq 0 \quad A \in \mathbf{R}^{p \times l} \tag{5.8}$$

zu finden, wobei die Ungleichungen komponentenweise zu verstehen sind. Falls $b = 0$ setzt man die zusätzliche Bedingung, daß die gefundene Lösung ungleich der trivialen $x = 0$ sein soll. Das System (5.8) wird als lösbar angenommen, d.h.

$$\exists x \in \mathbf{R}^l : Ax - b \geq 0 \quad \text{und} \quad x \neq 0 \quad \text{falls} \quad b = 0 \tag{5.9}$$

Das System (5.8) läßt sich als

$$\sum_{j=1}^{l} a_{ij} x_j - b_i \geq 0 \quad \forall i = 1, \ldots, p$$

schreiben. Die Lösungsmenge dieses Systems ist das konvexe Polytop

$$\Omega := \cap_{i=1}^{p} H_i$$

wobei H_i den i-ten geschlossenen Halbraum

$$H_i := \{x \in \mathbf{R}^l / \sum_{j=1}^{l} a_{ij} x_j - b_i \geq 0\}$$

bezeichnet. Wegen (5.9) ist Ω nicht leer.

Die Idee der Relaxations-Methode läßt sich intuitiv wie folgt beschreiben: Gegeben sei ein Punkt $P \notin \Omega$. Folgende Konstruktion liefert einen Punkt P_1, der näher zu Ω ist, als P : Da $P \notin \Omega$ gilt $P \notin H_i$ für ein $i = 1, \ldots, p$. Sei

$$\varpi_i := \{x \in \mathbf{R}^l / \sum_{j=1}^{l} a_{ij} x_j - b_i = 0\}$$

der Rand von H_i , P' der Punkt, der symmetrisch zu P bzgl. ϖ_i ist und Q die orthogonale Projektion von P auf ϖ_i. Für jeden Punkt $P_1 \neq P, P'$ auf dem linearen Segment PP' und jeden $S \in H_i$ gilt

$$\|P - S\|_2 > \|P_1 - S\|_2 \tag{5.10}$$

Einen algebraischen Beweis zu (5.10) findet man in *Agmon* [1]. Da $\Omega \subseteq H_i$ gilt (5.10) auch für alle $S \in \Omega$. Für P_1 hat man

$$P_1 = P + \lambda(Q - P), \quad \text{für ein} \quad \lambda, \quad 0 < \lambda < 2 \tag{5.11}$$

Für $\lambda = 2$ ist $P_1 = P'$ und (5.10) gilt als Gleichung für alle $S \in \Omega \cap \varpi_i$, falls welche existieren.

Die obigen Überlegungen legen folgenden Algorithmus nahe (s. *Motzkin & Schoenberg* [52]) :

Algorithmus 5.2 (Relaxations-Algorithmus) *Mit* $\text{dist}(P, H_i)$ *sei der Abstand eines Punktes P zum Unterraum H_i bezeichnet:*

$$\forall i = 1, \ldots, p : \text{dist}(P, H_i) = \min_{X \in H_i} \|P - X\|_2$$

Die Punktfolge $\{P_n\}_{n \in \mathbb{N}}$, definiert durch

$$
\begin{aligned}
\lambda &= \quad \text{beliebig mit} \quad 0 < \lambda \le 2 \\
P_1 &= \quad \text{beliebig} \\
P_{n+1} &= \begin{cases} P_n &: \quad P_n \in \Omega \\ P_n + \lambda(Q_{i_n} - P_n) &: \quad P_n \notin \Omega \end{cases}
\end{aligned}
\tag{5.12}
$$

heißt Relaxations-Algorithmus. Dabei ist Q_{i_n} die orthogonale Projektion von P_n auf den Rand ϖ_{i_n} von H_{i_n} und H_{i_n} ist so gewählt, daß

$$\text{dist}(P_n, H_{i_n}) = \max_i \text{dist}(P_n, H_i)$$

$\square$

Im folgenden wird mit k die Dimension des Polytops Ω , mit $\partial\Omega$ der Rand von Ω und mit $S^n(Q, d)$ die Sphäre im $\mathbb{R}^{n+1}$ mit Zentrum Q und Radius d.

Lemma 5.1 *Sei L_k ein affiner Unterraum von $\mathbb{R}^l$ der Dimension k, $0 \le k \le l - 1$ und P ein Punkt mit $P \notin L_k$. Sei*

$$X := \{B \in \mathbb{R}^l / \|B - S\|_2 = \|P - S\|_2, \quad \forall S \in L_k\} \tag{5.13}$$

Dann ist

$$X = S^{l-k-1}(Q, \|P - Q\|_2)$$

mit Q die orthogonale Projektion von P auf L_k

$\square$

Beweis : Siehe *Motzkin & Schoenberg* [52].

$\square$

Man sagt, daß L_k die *Axis* von $S^{l-k-1}(Q, \|P - Q\|_2)$ ist, da nach (5.13) L_k genau die Menge aller Punkte ist, die äquidistant zu allen Punkten von $S^{l-k-1}(Q, \|P - Q\|_2)$ liegen.

Sei nun L_k der kleinste affine Unterraum, der Ω enthält. Folgende zwei Sätze beschreiben das Verhalten des Relaxations-Algorithmus:

Satz 5.4 *Sei $k = l$, d.h. Ω ist in keiner Hyperebene von $\mathbb{R}^l$ enthalten. Für die durch (5.12) definierte Punktfolge $\{P_n\}_{n \in \mathbb{N}}$ unterscheide man zwei Fälle:*

1. Falls $0 < \lambda < 2$ dann

(a) entweder wird $\{P_n\}_{n\in\mathbb{N}}$ stationär, d.h.

$$\exists n_0 \in \mathbb{N} : P_n = P_{n_0}, \quad \forall n \geq n_0$$

(b) oder es gilt

$$\lim_{n\to\infty} P_n = L \in \partial\Omega$$

2. Falls $\lambda = 2$, wird $\{P_n\}_{n\in\mathbb{N}}$ stationär.

□

Beweis : Siehe *Motzkin & Schoenberg* [52].

□

Satz 5.5 *Sei* $k < l$, $\Omega \subseteq L_k$. *Für die durch (5.12) definierte Punktfolge* $\{P_n\}_{n\in\mathbb{N}}$ *unterscheide man zwei Fälle:*

1. *Falls* $0 < \lambda < 2$ *dann*

   (a) *entweder wird* $\{P_n\}_{n\in\mathbb{N}}$ *stationär*

   (b) *oder es gilt*

   $$\lim_{n\to\infty} P_n = L \in \Omega$$

2. *Falls* $\lambda = 2$, *dann*

   (a) *entweder wird* $\{P_n\}_{n\in\mathbb{N}}$ *stationär*

   (b) *oder es existiert ein* n_0, *so daß die Punkte* P_n, $n \geq n_0$ *auf einer Sphäre* S^{l-k-1} *liegen, die* L_k *als Axis hat.*

□

Beweis : Siehe *Motzkin & Schoenberg* [52].

□

Der Relaxations-Algorithmus ist in der Lage, für Systeme der Form

$$Aw - b \geq 0$$

eine Lösung zu finden. Er kann auch zur Lösung von Systemen der Form

$$Aw > 0$$

eingesetzt werden, denn es gilt folgendes

Lemma 5.2 *Folgende Aussagen sind äquivalent:*

1. $\exists w_* : Aw_* > 0$

2. $\forall b > 0 \quad \exists w' : Aw' - b \geq 0$

(Die Ungleichungen sind komponentenweise zu verstehen).

$\square$

Beweis : **2)** $\Rightarrow$ **1):** Wähle $b = (1, \ldots, 1)^\top$. Es folgt

$$\exists w' : \sum_j a_{ij} w_j' - 1 \geq 0 \quad \forall i$$

also

$$\exists w' : \sum_j a_{ij} w_j' > 0 \quad \forall i$$

und 1) folgt mit $w_* = w'$.

1) $\Rightarrow$ **2):** Sei $b_* := Aw_*$. Dann ist

$$b_* > 0 \quad \text{und} \quad Aw_* = b_*$$

Sei b beliebiger Vektor mit $b > 0$. Man definiere c, d durch

$$c := \min_i b_{*i}, \quad d := \max_i b_i$$

wobei x_i die i-te Koordinate von x bedeutet, sowie die Vektoren $\tilde{c}, \tilde{d}$ durch

$$\tilde{c} = (c, \ldots, c)^\top, \quad \tilde{d} = (d, \ldots, d)^\top$$

Es ist klar, daß (komponentenweise)

$$b_* - \tilde{c} \geq 0 \quad \text{und} \quad \tilde{d} - b \geq 0$$

Nun ist

$$b_* - \tilde{c} \geq 0 \Rightarrow Aw_* - \tilde{c} \geq 0 \quad \Rightarrow \quad \frac{d}{c} Aw_* - \frac{d}{c} \tilde{c} \geq 0 \Rightarrow$$

$$\Rightarrow A(\frac{d}{c} w_*) - d(1, \ldots, 1)^\top \geq 0 \quad \Rightarrow \quad Aw' - \tilde{d} \geq 0$$

mit $w' := \frac{d}{c} w_*$. Da $\tilde{d} - b \geq 0$ folgt

$$Aw' - b \geq 0$$

$\square$

Zur Lösung des Systems

$$Aw > 0$$

genügt es also den Relaxations-Algorithmus mit beliebigem $b > 0$ einzusetzen. Aus den Sätzen 5.4 und 5.5 folgt dann, daß der Relaxations-Algorithmus (mit Ausnahme vom Fall 2b)) eine Lernregel im Sinne von Def. 3.1 definiert, die *Relaxations-Lernregel*.

Da es gilt

$$\text{dist}(P_n, H_{i_n}) = \text{dist}(P_n, \varpi_{i_n})$$

und aus der linearen Algebra

$$\text{dist}(P_n, \varpi_{i_n}) = \frac{|a_{i_n}^{\mathsf{T}} P_n - b_{i_n}|}{\|a_{i_n}\|_2} \tag{5.14}$$

folgt für Q_{i_n}, P_n in (5.12)

$$Q_{i_n} - P_n = \text{dist}(P_n, H_{i_n}) \frac{a_{i_n}}{\|a_{i_n}\|_2} = \frac{|a_{i_n}^{\mathsf{T}} P_n - b_{i_n}|}{\|a_{i_n}\|_2^2} a_{i_n}$$

mit a_{i_n} die i_n-te Spalte von A^{T}. Man kann also die Relaxations-Lernregel wie folgt schreiben (hier wird (5.12) mit Vektoren geschrieben):

$$
\begin{aligned}
\lambda &= \quad \text{beliebig mit} \quad 0 < \lambda \leq 2 \\
w_1 &= \quad \text{beliebig} \\
w_{n+1} &= \begin{cases} w_n + \lambda \dfrac{|a_{i_n}^{\mathsf{T}} w_n - b_{i_n}|}{\|a_{i_n}\|_2^2} a_{i_n} & : \quad a_{i_n}^{\mathsf{T}} w_n - b_{i_n} < 0 \\ w_n & : \quad \text{sonst} \end{cases}
\end{aligned}
\tag{5.15}
$$

s. *Duda & Hart* [16] S. 148.

Dies kann vereinfacht werden: Mit $\Lambda := \text{diag}(\|a_1\|_2^{-1}, \ldots, \|a_p\|_2^{-1})$ folgt aus Lemma 5.2

$$\exists w : Aw > 0 \Leftrightarrow \forall b > 0 \quad \exists w' : Aw' - b \geq 0$$

$$\Leftrightarrow \forall b > 0 \quad \exists w' : \Lambda Aw' - \Lambda b \geq 0$$

$$\Leftrightarrow \forall b > 0 \quad \exists w' : \tilde{A} w' - \Lambda b \geq 0$$

$$\Leftrightarrow \forall b' > 0 \quad \exists w'' : \tilde{A} w'' - b' \geq 0$$

mit $\tilde{A} := \Lambda A$. Man beachte, daß die Zeilen von $\tilde{A}$ — als Vektoren aufgefaßt — die Länge 1 haben. Falls also das System $Aw > 0$ lösbar ist, kann man den Relaxationsalgorithmus auf das System

$$\tilde{A} w'' - b' \geq 0$$

anwenden, wobei $b' = (1, \ldots, 1)^{\mathsf{T}}$ und $\tilde{A} = \Lambda A$ sind. Die gefundene Lösung w'' wird auch eine Lösung von $Aw > 0$ sein. Man kann also schreiben

$$
\begin{aligned}
\lambda &= \quad \text{beliebig mit} \quad 0 < \lambda \leq 2 \\
a'_i &= \quad \frac{a_i}{\|a_i\|_2} \\
w_1 &= \quad \text{beliebig} \\
w_{n+1} &= \begin{cases} w_n + \lambda |a'^{\mathsf{T}}_{i_n} w_n - 1| a'_{i_n} & : \quad a'^{\mathsf{T}}_{i_n} w_n - 1 < 0 \\ w_n & : \quad \text{sonst} \end{cases}
\end{aligned}
\tag{5.16}
$$

Diese Form, die von manchen Autoren bevorzugt wird, sowie (5.15) hat eine große Ähnlichkeit zur Form der Perceptron- bzw. Delta-Regel.

Für den Fall, daß die Relaxations-Lernregel (5.15) stationär wird, also eine Lösung von $Aw - b \geq 0$ in endlich vielen Schritten n_0 erreicht, kann man folgenden Satz beweisen:

Satz 5.6 *Das System $Aw > 0$ sei lösbar. Sei $b \in \mathbb{R}^p$, $b > 0$ gegeben. Ferner sei die durch (5.15) definierte Relaxations-Lernregel nach endlich vielen Schritten stationär, d.h.*

$$\exists n_0 \in \mathbb{N} : w_n = w_{n_0} \quad \forall n \geq n_0$$

Dann gilt :

$$\exists \overline{w} : n_0 < \frac{\|w_1 - \overline{w}\|_2^2}{\beta^2} + 1 \tag{5.17}$$

mit

$$a_i \quad : \quad \textit{i-te Spalte von} \quad A^\top$$
$$\varrho_n \quad = \quad \lambda \frac{|a_{i_n}^\top w_n - b_{i_n}|}{\|a_{i_n}\|_2}$$
$$\varrho_{min} \quad = \quad \min_{n \in \{1,...,n_0\}} \{\varrho_n\}$$
$$\varrho_{max} \quad = \quad \max_{n \in \{1,...,n_0\}} \{\varrho_n\}$$
$$c_1, c_2 \quad : \quad \textit{beliebig, mit} \quad 0 < c_1 \leq \varrho_{min} \leq \varrho_{max} \leq c_2$$
$$\beta \quad = \quad \sqrt{c_1 c_2}$$
$$\gamma \quad = \quad \frac{c_1 + c_2}{2}$$

$$\min_{i \in \{1,...,p\}} \left\{ \frac{\overline{w}^\top a_i - b_i}{\|a_i\|_2} \right\} \geq \gamma \tag{5.18}$$

$\square$

Beweis (Analog zum Satz 5.3): Aus Lemma 5.2 folgt, da $Aw > 0$ lösbar ist, daß ein $\overline{w}$ existiert, das (5.18) genügt. (Die Berechnung von einem solchen $\overline{w}$ folgt im Lemma 5.3). Für beliebiges $n < n_0$ gilt

$$\|w_{n+1} - \overline{w}\|_2^2 =$$
$$= \|w_n - \overline{w}\|_2^2 + 2(w_n - \overline{w})^\top \varrho_n \frac{a_{i_n}}{\|a_{i_n}\|_2} + \varrho_n^2 =$$
$$= \|w_n - \overline{w}\|_2^2 + 2\varrho_n \frac{w_n^\top a_{i_n}}{\|a_{i_n}\|_2} - 2\varrho_n \frac{\overline{w}^\top a_{i_n}}{\|a_{i_n}\|_2} + \varrho_n^2 <$$
$$< \|w_n - \overline{w}\|_2^2 + 2\varrho_n \frac{b_{i_n}}{\|a_{i_n}\|_2} - 2\varrho_n \frac{\overline{w}^\top a_{i_n}}{\|a_{i_n}\|_2} + \varrho_n^2 =$$
$$= \|w_n - \overline{w}\|_2^2 - 2\varrho_n \frac{\overline{w}^\top a_{i_n} - b_{i_n}}{\|a_{i_n}\|_2} + \varrho_n^2 \leq$$
$$\leq \|w_n - \overline{w}\|_2^2 - 2\varrho_n \gamma + \varrho_n^2 \leq$$
$$\leq \|w_n - \overline{w}\|_2^2 - \beta^2 \tag{5.19}$$

da aus der Wahl von i_n gilt $w_n^\top a_{i_n} < b_{i_n}$ $\forall n < n_0$ und aus

$$0 < c_1 \le \varrho_{min} \le \varrho_n \le \varrho_{max} \le c_2$$

folgt

$$\varrho_n^2 - (c_1 + c_2)\varrho_n + c_1 c_2 \le 0 \Rightarrow \varrho_n^2 - 2\gamma\varrho_n + \beta^2 \le 0$$

Durch n-malige Anwendung von (5.19) folgt

$$0 \le \|w_{n+1} - \overline{w}\|_2^2 < \|w_1 - \overline{w}\|_2^2 - n\beta^2 \Rightarrow n < \frac{\|w_1 - \overline{w}\|_2^2}{\beta^2} \quad \forall n < n_0$$

und daraus (5.17) für $n = n_0 - 1$.

$\square$

Im folgenden Lemma wird ein $\overline{w}$ berechnet:

Lemma 5.3 *Folgendes $\overline{w}$ genügt (5.18):*

$$\overline{w} = \frac{\lambda e_2(\|w_1 - \frac{d}{\alpha}w_*\|_2 + \frac{d}{\alpha}\|w_*\|_2 + \frac{d}{e_1}) + d}{\alpha} w_*$$

$$mit :$$

w_* : *eine Lösung von* $Aw > 0$

$d = \max_{i \in \{1,\dots,p\}}\{b_i\}$

$\alpha = \min_{i \in \{1,\dots,p\}}\{(Aw_*)_i\} = \min_{i \in \{1,\dots,p\}}\{a_i^\top w_*\}$

a_i : *i-te Spalte von* $A^\top$

$e_1 = \min_{i \in \{1,\dots,p\}}\{\|a_i\|_2\}$

$e_2 = \max_{i \in \{1,\dots,p\}}\{\|a_i\|_2\}$

$c_1 = \varrho_{min}$

$c_2 = \varrho_{max}$ \hfill (5.20)

$\square$

Beweis : Aus (5.10) folgt

$$\|w_n - w'\|_2 \le \|w_1 - w'\|_2 \tag{5.21}$$

mit $w' \in \Omega$, also eine Lösung von $Aw - b \ge 0$. Aus (5.21):

$$\|w_n\|_2 - \|w'\|_2 \le \|w_1 - w'\|_2 \Rightarrow \|w_n\|_2 \le \|w_1 - w'\|_2 + \|w'\|_2 \tag{5.22}$$

Man kann

$$w' = \frac{d}{\alpha}w_*$$

setzen (s. Beweis von Lemma 5.2). Nun ist

$$\varrho_n = \lambda \frac{|a_{i_n}^{\top} w_n - b_{i_n}|}{\|a_{i_n}\|_2} \leq \lambda \frac{\|a_{i_n}\|_2 \|w_n\|_2 + |b_{i_n}|}{\|a_{i_n}\|_2} = \lambda(\|w_n\|_2 + \frac{|b_{i_n}|}{\|a_{i_n}\|_2})$$

und aus (5.22)

$$\varrho_{max} \leq \lambda(\|w_1 - w'\|_2 + \|w'\|_2 + \frac{d}{e_1}) \qquad (5.23)$$

Sei

$$c_2 = \varrho_{max} \qquad (5.24)$$

Da $c_1 \leq c_2$ folgt

$$\gamma = \frac{c_1 + c_2}{2} \leq c_2 = \varrho_{max}$$

Mit $c_2 = \varrho_{max}$ und $0 < c_1 \leq \varrho_{min}$ genügt es also, ein $\overline{w}$ so zu wählen, daß

$$\frac{\overline{w}^{\top} a_i - b_i}{\|a_i\|_2} \geq \varrho_{max} \quad \forall i = 1, \ldots, p$$

Beste Abschätzung für n_0 erhält man bei $c_1 = \varrho_{min}$. Aus (5.23) folgt nun, daß es genügt, ein $\overline{w}$ zu wählen, so daß es gilt:

$$\frac{\overline{w}^{\top} a_i - b_i}{\|a_i\|_2} \geq \lambda(\|w_1 - w'\|_2 + \|w'\|_2 + \frac{d}{e_1}) \Rightarrow$$

$$\Rightarrow \overline{w}^{\top} a_i \geq \lambda \|a_i\|_2 (\|w_1 - w'\|_2 + \|w'\|_2 + \frac{d}{e_1}) + b_i \quad \forall i = 1, \ldots, p$$

Aus dem Beweis von Lemma 5.2 folgt, daß man

$$\overline{w} = \frac{\max\limits_{i=1,\ldots,p} \{\lambda \|a_i\|_2 (\|w_1 - w'\|_2 + \|w'\|_2 + \frac{d}{e_1}) + b_i\}}{\min\limits_{i=1,\ldots,p} \{(Aw_*)_i\}} w_*$$

wählen kann. Also

$$\overline{w} = \frac{\lambda e_2 (\|w_1 - \frac{d}{\alpha} w_*\|_2 + \frac{d}{\alpha} \|w_*\|_2 + \frac{d}{e_1}) + d}{\alpha} w_*$$

$\square$

5.3 Die Ho-Kashyap-Lernregel

Die in diesem Abschnitt vorgestellte *Ho-Kashyap-Methode* zur Lösung eines Systems linearer Ungleichungen ist eine Methode des steilsten Abstiegs. Ihre Merkmale sind schnelle Konvergenz und die Möglichkeit zu erkennen, ob das System unlösbar ist.

Anstatt mit dem Problem

'Finde w , so daß $Aw > 0$ '

befaßt sich die Ho-Kashyap-Methode mit dem äquivalenten

'Finde w, b, so daß $Aw = b$ und $b > 0$',

das wiederum äquivalent zu

'Finde w, b mit $b > 0$, so daß $J := \|Aw - b\|_2^2$ minimal wird'

ist.

Intuitiv kann man die Ho-Kashyap-Methode wie folgt beschrieben: Da

$$\frac{\partial J}{\partial w} = 2A^\top(Aw - b)$$
$$\frac{\partial J}{\partial b} = 2(b - Aw)$$

gilt, ist ein optimales w für gegebenes b Lösung von

$$\frac{\partial J}{\partial w} = 0$$

also von

$$A^\top Aw - A^\top b = 0$$

Daher setzt man

$$w = A^+ b$$

mit A^+ die Moore-Penrose-Inverse (denn $A^\top AA^+ = A^\top$, s. Lemma 5.5(1)). Für festes w wird b in Richtung des steilsten Abstiegs, unter Berücksichtigung von $b > 0$, geändert d.h. man addiert nur diejenigen Komponenten von $-\frac{\partial J}{\partial b}$, die positiv sind. Mit den Bezeichnungen für $x \in R^n$

$$|x| = (|x_1|, \ldots, |x_n|)^\top \in R^n$$
$$x_+ = x + |x| \tag{5.25}$$

erhält man folgenden (s. [27])

Algorithmus 5.3 (Ho-Kashyap-Algorithmus) *Die Folge* $\{w_n, b_n\}_{n \in N}$ *definiert durch*

$$\varrho = beliebig\ mit \quad 0 < \varrho < 1$$
$$b_1 = beliebig\ mit \quad b_1 > 0$$
$$w_1 = A^+ b_1$$
$$b_{n+1} = b_n + \varrho(Aw_n - b_n)_+$$
$$w_{n+1} = A^+ b_{n+1}$$

heißt Ho-Kashyap-Algorithmus

$\square$

Eine äquivalente Schreibweise des Ho-Kashyap-Algorithmus ist

$$
\begin{aligned}
\varrho &= \text{beliebig mit} \quad 0 < \varrho < 1 \\
b_1 &= \text{beliebig mit} \quad b_1 > 0 \\
w_1 &= A^+ b_1 \\
r_n &= A w_n - b_n \\
b_{n+1} &= b_n + \varrho r_{n+} \\
w_{n+1} &= w_n + \varrho A^+ r_{n+}
\end{aligned}
\tag{5.26}
$$

Bemerkung : Der Vektor $r_n = A w_n - b_n$ hat die Richtung von $-\frac{\partial J}{\partial b}$. Der Vektor r_{n+} hat als Komponenten

$$
(r_{n+})_i = \begin{cases} 2(r_n)_i & : \quad (r_n)_i > 0 \\ 0 & : \quad \text{sonst} \end{cases}
$$

Da in der Literatur das Verhalten des Ho-Kashyap-Algorithmus unklar dargestellt wird, wird er im folgenden ausfürlich untersucht. Folgende Lemmata sind dazu nötig:

Lemma 5.4 *Für alle* $x \in \mathbb{R}^n$ *gilt* $2x^\top x_+ = x_+^\top x_+$

$\square$

Beweis : Aus (5.25) folgt leicht

$$
(x_+ - 2|x|)_i = \begin{cases} 0 & : \quad x_{+i} \geq 0 \\ -2|x_i| & : \quad \text{sonst} \end{cases}
$$

also $x_+^\top (x_+ - 2|x|) = 0$ und daraus

$$
x_+^\top x_+ + x_+^\top (x_+ - 2|x|) = x_+^\top x_+ \Rightarrow 2x_+^\top x_+ - 2x_+^\top |x| = x_+^\top x_+ \Rightarrow
$$
$$
\Rightarrow 2x_+^\top (x_+ - |x|) = x_+^\top x_+ \Rightarrow 2x_+^\top x = x_+^\top x_+
$$

da per Definition $x_+ = x + |x|$.

$\square$

Lemma 5.5 *Es gilt*

1. $A^\top r_n = 0 \quad \forall n \in \mathbb{N}$

2. $AA^+ r_n = 0 \quad \forall n \in \mathbb{N}$

$\square$

Beweis : Aus (5.26) : $r_n = (AA^+ - I)b_n$. Nach Korollar 3.5 in *Albert* [2] ist AA^+ die orthogonale Projektion auf $R(A)$ und $I - AA^+$ die orthogonale Projektion auf $N(A^\top)$.

1. Es folgt $r_n = -(I - AA^+)b_n \in N(A^\top)$ und daraus die Behauptung.

2. $AA^+ r_n = -AA^+(I - AA^+)b_n$. Da $(I - AA^+)b_n \in N(A^\top)$ und AA^+ die orthogonale Projektion auf $R(A)$ ist, folgt die Behauptung direkt aus Lemma 3.1.

$\square$

Lemma 5.6 *Sei $Q \in \mathbb{R}^{n \times n}$ eine symmetrische, positiv-definite Matrix. Es gilt für alle $x \in \mathbb{R}^n$*

$$x^\top Q x \geq \lambda \|x\|_2^2$$

wobei $\lambda > 0$ der kleinste Eigenwert von Q ist.

$\square$

Beweis : Aus der linearen Algebra: Da Q symmetrisch ist, hat n reele Eigenwerte $\lambda_1, \ldots, \lambda_n$ und es existiert eine Matrix C , so daß

$$C^\top Q C = \mathrm{diag}(\lambda_1, \ldots, \lambda_n) =: \Lambda \quad \text{und} \quad CC^\top = I$$

Also

$$x^\top Q x = y^\top C^\top Q C y = y^\top \Lambda y = \sum_{i=1}^{n} \lambda_i y_i^2$$

mit $y := C^\top x$. Da Q positiv-definit ist, folgt $\lambda_i > 0$, $\forall i = 1, \ldots, n$. Daraus folgt

$$x^\top Q x \geq \lambda \sum_{i=1}^{n} y_i^2 = \lambda \|y\|_2^2 = \lambda x^\top C C^\top x = \lambda x^\top x = \lambda \|x\|_2^2$$

mit $\lambda > 0$ den kleinsten Eigenwert von Q.

$\square$

Bemerkung: Das Funktional

$$\| \cdot \|_Q : \mathbb{R}^n \to \mathbb{R}_0^+ : x \mapsto \|x\|_Q = \sqrt{x^\top Q x}$$

ist eine Norm, dann und nur dann, wenn Q positiv-definit ist, siehe *Golub & Van Loan* [19], Problem P2.1-7, S. 13.

Folgendes Lemma wird in *Ho & Kashyap* [27] unklar formuliert:

Lemma 5.7 .

1. *Es gilt für alle $n \in \mathbb{N}$*

   (a) *entweder $r_n = 0$*

   (b) *oder $r_n \ngeq 0$*

2. *Falls $Aw > 0$ lösbar ist, dann gilt für alle $n \in \mathbb{N}$*

(a) entweder $r_n = 0$

(b) oder $r_{n+} \neq 0$

$\square$

Bemerkungen :

1. Da $r_n \geq 0$ komponentenweise zu verstehen ist, bedeutet $r_n \not\geq 0$ *nicht* $r_n < 0$.

2. Obiges Lemma garantiert, daß, falls $Aw > 0$ lösbar ist und der Algorithmus niemals eine Lösung $\{w_{n^*}, b_{n^*}\}$ mit $Aw_{n^*} = b_{n^*}$ erreicht, die Folge $\{w_n, b_n\}_{n \in \mathbb{N}}$ nie stationär wird (s. (5.26)).

Beweis vom Lemma 5.7 : In beiden Fällen durch Widerspruch:

1) Sei $r_n \geq 0$ und $r_n \neq 0$ für ein $n \in \mathbb{N}$. Dann gilt

$$r_n^{\top} b_n > 0 \tag{5.27}$$

da aus Konstruktion $b_n > 0$. Aber wegen (5.26)

$$r_n = Aw_n - b_n = (AA^+ - I)b_n$$

und daher

$$r_n^{\top} b_n = b_n^{\top}(AA^+ - I)^{\top} b_n = b_n^{\top}(AA^+ - I)b_n \leq 0$$

da AA^+ symmetrisch ist (s. A(3) Satz 3.4) und $AA^+ - I$ nach Lemma 3.3 negativsemidefinit ist. Dies ist ein Widerspruch zu (5.27).

2) Angenommen

$$r_{n_0} \neq 0 \quad \text{und} \quad r_{n_0+} = 0 \quad \text{für ein} \quad n_0 \in \mathbb{N} \tag{5.28}$$

Da $Aw > 0$ lösbar ist, existieren w^*, b^* derart, daß

$$Aw^* = b^* > 0$$

Aus (5.28) folgt

$$r_{n_0}^{\top} b^* < 0 \tag{5.29}$$

Aber aus Lemma 5.5:

$$A^{\top} r_n = 0 \quad \forall n \in \mathbb{N}$$

Also

$$A^{\top} r_{n_0} = 0 \Rightarrow w^{*\top} A^{\top} r_{n_0} = 0 \Rightarrow b^{*\top} r_{n_0} = r_{n_0}^{\top} b^* = 0$$

Dies ist ein Widerspruch zu (5.29).

$\square$

Lemma 5.8 *Seien*

$$V(r_n) := \|r_n\|_2^2$$
$$\Delta V(r_n) := V(r_{n+1}) - V(r_n)$$

Es gilt

$$\Delta V(r_n) = -r_{n+}^\top (\varrho^2 AA^+ + \varrho(1 - \varrho)I)r_{n+}$$

$\square$

Beweis : Aus (5.26) folgt

$$r_{n+1} = r_n + \varrho(AA^+ - I)r_{n+}$$

Also

$$\Delta V(r_n) = \|r_{n+1}\|_2^2 - \|r_n\|_2^2 = 2\varrho r_n^\top (AA^+ - I)r_{n+} + \varrho^2 r_{n+}^\top (AA^+ - I)^\top (AA^+ - I)r_{n+}$$

Da nach Korollar 3.5 in *Albert* [2] $I - AA^+$ eine orthogonale Projektion ist, folgt (s. Def. 3.5)

$$(AA^+ - I)^\top (AA^+ - I) = (I - AA^+)^\top (I - AA^+) = (I - AA^+)(I - AA^+) = I - AA^+$$

Also

$$\Delta V(r_n) = 2\varrho r_n^\top (AA^+ - I)r_{n+} + \varrho^2 r_{n+}^\top (I - AA^+)r_{n+} =$$
$$= 2\varrho r_n^\top AA^+ r_{n+} - 2\varrho r_n^\top r_{n+} + \varrho^2 r_{n+}^\top (I - AA^+)r_{n+}$$

Nun ist

$$2\varrho r_n^\top AA^+ r_{n+} = 2\varrho((AA^+)^\top r_n)^\top r_{n+} = 2\varrho(AA^+ r_n)^\top r_{n+} = 0$$

weil $AA^+ r_n = 0$ aus Lemma 5.5. Ferner ist aus Lemma 5.4

$$-2\varrho r_n^\top r_{n+} = -\varrho r_{n+}^\top r_{n+}$$

Zusammenfassend

$$\Delta V(r_n) = r_{n+}^\top (-\varrho I)r_{n+} + r_{n+}^\top \varrho^2 (I - AA^+)r_{n+} = -r_{n+}^\top (\varrho^2 AA^+ + \varrho(1 - \varrho)I)r_{n+}$$

$\square$

Lemma 5.9 *Falls* $\Delta V(r_{n_0}) = 0$, *für ein* $n_0 \in N$,

1.

$$\begin{aligned} w_n &= w_{n_0}, \quad \forall n \geq n_0 \\ b_n &= b_{n_0}, \quad \forall n \geq n_0 \\ r_n &= r_{n_0}, \quad \forall n \geq n_0 \end{aligned} \qquad (5.30)$$

2. *Falls $Aw > 0$ lösbar ist, gilt zusätzlich*

$$r_{n_0} = 0$$

$\square$

Beweis :

1. Die Matrix AA^+ ist positiv-semidefinit (s. Lemma 3.3). Für $0 < \varrho < 1$ ist die Matrix $\varrho(1 - \varrho)I$ positiv-definit. Daher ist für $0 < \varrho < 1$ die Matrix $(\varrho^2 AA^+ + \varrho(1 - \varrho)I)$ positiv-definit und aus $\Delta V(r_{n_0}) = 0$ und Lemma 5.8 folgt $r_{n_0 +} = 0$. Die Gl. (5.30) folgen nun direkt aus (5.26).

2. Das System $Aw > 0$ sei lösbar und es gelte $\Delta V(r_{n_0}) = 0$. Da es $r_{n_0 +} = 0$ gelten muß (s. (1) oben), folgt die Behauptung aus Lemma 5.7.

$\square$

Lemma 5.10 *Es gilt:*

$$\exists \lambda > 0 : \quad \forall n \in \mathbb{N} \quad \Delta V(r_n) \leq -\lambda \|r_{n+}\|_2^2$$

$\square$

Beweis: Aus Lemma 5.8, der Positiv-Definitheit der symmetrischen Matrix $(\varrho^2 AA^+ + \varrho(1 - \varrho)I)$ (s. Lemma 5.9) und Lemma 5.6 folgt

$$\Delta V(r_n) = -r_{n+}^\top (\varrho^2 AA^+ + \varrho(1 - \varrho)I)r_{n+} \leq -\lambda \|r_{n+}\|_2^2$$

mit $\lambda > 0$ den kleinsten Eigenwert von $\varrho^2 AA^+ + \varrho(1 - \varrho)I$.

$\square$

Bemerkung: Aus der Konstruktion von r_{n+} folgt

$$r_{n+} = C_n r_n$$

mit

$$C_n = [c_{ij}^n] \in \mathbb{R}^{p \times p}$$
$$c_{ij}^n = \begin{cases} 2 & : (r_n)_i \geq 0 \quad \text{und} \quad i = j \\ 0 & : \text{sonst} \end{cases}$$

In *Ho & Kashyap* [27] wird ohne Beweis behauptet, daß, falls $\Delta V(r_n) < 0$

$$\Delta V(r_n) \leq -\lambda(n) \|r_n\|_2^2 = -\lambda(n) V(r_n) \tag{5.31}$$

mit $\lambda(n) > 0$ den kleinsten positiven Eigenwert von $C_n^\top (\varrho^2 AA^+ + \varrho(1 - \varrho)I)C_n$. Da aus Lemma 5.7 $r_n \not\geq 0$, hat die Diagonalmatrix C_n mindestens eine Null auf der Diagonale, ist sie aber im Falle $\Delta V(r_n) < 0$ wegen Lemma 5.8 stets ungleich Null. Aus der Positiv-Definitheit der Matrix $(\varrho^2 AA^+ + \varrho(1 - \varrho)I)$ (s. Lemma 5.9) folgt, daß die Matrix $C_n^\top (\varrho^2 AA^+ + \varrho(1 - \varrho)I)C_n$ positiv-*semidefinit* ist. Lemma 5.6 gilt für positiv-semidefinite Matrizen i. allg. nicht, daher ist es unklar, warum (5.31) gelten soll.

Definition 5.1 *Ein Vektor $u \in \mathbb{R}^n$ ist ein* Fixpunkt *von $f : \mathbb{R}^n \to \mathbb{R}^n$, falls $f(u) = u$.*

□

Definition 5.2 *Sei $u \in \mathbb{R}^n$ und $d > 0$. Die* offene Kugel *mit Zentrum u und Radius d ist die Menge*

$$B(u, d) = \{v \in \mathbb{R}^n : \quad \|v - u\|_2 < d\}$$

Sei v ein Fixpunkt von f. Dann heißt v stabil, falls für jede Kugel $B(v, \epsilon)$ eine Kugel $B(v, \delta)$ existiert so, daß, wenn $u \in B(v, \delta)$, dann $f^n(u) \in B(v, \epsilon)$ für alle $n \in \mathbb{N}$. Hier ist $f^n(u) = \underbrace{f(\cdots(f(f(u)))\cdots)}_{n \text{ Mal}}$.

Falls es zusätzlich eine Kugel $B(v, d)$ existiert so, daß $f^n(u) \to v$ für $n \to \infty$ für alle $u \in B(v, d)$, dann heißt v asymptotisch stabil.

□

Definition 5.3 *Sei v ein Fixpunkt von f. Eine reel-wertige, stetige Funktion V in einer Kugel B um v heißt* Lyapunov-Funktion *für f in v, falls $V(v) = 0$, $V(u) > 0$ für $u \neq v$ in B und*

$$\Delta V(u) \equiv V(f(u)) - V(u) \leq 0 \tag{5.32}$$

für alle $u \in B$. Falls die Ungleichung (5.32) für $u \neq v$ strikt gilt, dann ist V eine strikte Lyapunov-Funktion *für f in v.*

□

Es gilt folgender

Satz 5.7 (Stabilitätskriterium von Lyapunov für diskrete Systeme) *Sei B eine Kugel um v, v ein Fixpunkt von f und f stetig in B.*

Falls es eine Lyapunov-Funktion V für f in v gibt, dann ist v stabil.

Falls es eine strikte Lyapunov-Funktion V für f in v gibt, dann ist v asymptotisch stabil.

□

Beweis: Siehe *Kelley & Peterson* [35] S. 177.

□

Lemma 5.11 *a) Falls*

$$r_{n+} \neq 0 \quad \forall n \in \mathbb{N}$$

dann

$$\lim_{n \to \infty} r_{n+} = 0$$

b) Falls das Systen $Aw > 0$ lösbar ist, gilt zusätzlich

$$\lim_{n \to \infty} r_n = 0$$

□

Beweis : **a)** Sei

$$r_{n+} \neq 0 \quad \forall n \in \mathbb{N} \tag{5.33}$$

Daher

$$r_n \neq 0 \quad \forall n \in \mathbb{N} \tag{5.34}$$

und aus Lemma 5.8 und dem Beweis von Lemma 5.9(1) folgt

$$\forall n \in \mathbb{N} : \Delta V(r_n) < 0, \quad V(r_n) > 0 \tag{5.35}$$

Die Folge $\{V(r_n)\}_{n \in \mathbb{N}}$ ist also beschränkt und monoton fallend, daher konvergent. Durch Grenzübergang erhält man

$$\lim_{n \to \infty} \Delta V(r_n) = 0 \tag{5.36}$$

Für die Folge $\{r_{n+}\}_{n \in \mathbb{N}}$ gilt

$$\|r_{n+}\|_2 < 2\|r_n\|_2 \quad \forall n \in \mathbb{N}$$

(ohne Gleichheit wegen Lemma 5.7(1)). Sie ist also beschränkt, da $\{r_n\}_{n \in \mathbb{N}}$ beschränkt ist (s. (5.35)). Sei $\{r_{s_n+}\}_{n \in \mathbb{N}}$ eine konvergente Unterfolge von $\{r_{n+}\}_{n \in \mathbb{N}}$. Aus (5.36) und Lemma 5.8 folgt

$$-(\lim_{n \to \infty} r_{s_n+})^\top (\varrho^2 A A^+ + \varrho(1 - \varrho)I)(\lim_{n \to \infty} r_{s_n+}) = 0$$

und aus der Positiv-Definitheit der Matrix $(\varrho^2 A A^+ + \varrho(1 - \varrho)I)$ (s. Beweis von Lemma 5.9(1))

$$\lim_{n \to \infty} r_{s_n+} = 0$$

Da dies für alle konvergenten Unterfolgen $\{r_{s_n+}\}_{n \in \mathbb{N}}$ von $\{r_{n+}\}_{n \in \mathbb{N}}$ gelten muß, folgt

$$\lim_{n \to \infty} r_{n+} = 0$$

b) Das System $Aw > 0$ sei nun lösbar:

$$\exists w^*, b^* : Aw^* = b^* > 0$$

Aus Lemma 5.5:

$$A^\top r_n = 0 \quad \forall n \in \mathbb{N}$$

Also

$$w^{*\top} A^\top r_n = 0 \Rightarrow b^{*\top} r_n = 0 \quad \forall n \in \mathbb{N} \tag{5.37}$$

Sei $\{r_{k_n}\}_{n \in \mathbb{N}}$ eine konvergente Unterfolge von $\{r_n\}_{n \in \mathbb{N}}$ ($\{r_n\}_{n \in \mathbb{N}}$ ist beschränkt, s. (5.35)) mit

$$\lim_{n \to \infty} r_{k_n} = \bar{r}$$

Aus (5.37)

$$\lim_{n \to \infty} b^{*\top} r_n = 0 \Rightarrow \lim_{n \to \infty} b^{*\top} r_{k_n} = 0 \Rightarrow b^{*\top} \bar{r} = 0 \tag{5.38}$$

Sei nun
$$\bar{r} \neq 0$$
Da aus a)
$$\lim_{n\to\infty} r_{k_n+} = 0$$
muß
$$\bar{r}_+ = (\lim_{n\to\infty} r_{k_n})_+ = \lim_{n\to\infty} r_{k_n+} = 0$$
gelten. Daher hat $\bar{r}$ keine positive Komponenten, also
$$b^{*\mathsf{T}}\bar{r} < 0$$
Dies ist ein Widerspruch zu (5.38). Für jede konvergente Unterfolge $\{r_{k_n}\}_{n\in\mathbb{N}}$ von $\{r_n\}_{n\in\mathbb{N}}$ muß also
$$\lim_{n\to\infty} r_{k_n} = 0$$
gelten. Daher
$$\lim_{n\to\infty} r_n = 0$$

$\square$

Lemma 5.12 *Falls*
$$\lim_{n\to\infty} r_n = 0 \tag{5.39}$$
dann gilt
$$\exists n^* \in \mathbb{N} : Aw_n > 0 \quad \forall n \geq n^*$$

$\square$

Beweis : Aus (5.26)
$$b_{n+1} - b_n = \varrho r_{n+} \geq 0$$
Durch Induktion erhält man
$$b_n - b_1 \geq 0 \quad \forall n \in \mathbb{N} \tag{5.40}$$
Aus (5.39)
$$\exists n^* : \|r_n\|_2^2 < b_{min}^2 \quad \forall n \geq n^*$$
mit $b_{min} := \min_i b_{1i}$. Es folgt
$$\|r_n\|_2 < b_{min} \quad \forall n \geq n^*$$
$$\Rightarrow |(r_n)_i| < b_{min} \quad \forall n \geq n^*$$
$$\Rightarrow r_n + b_1 > 0 \quad \forall n \geq n^* \tag{5.41}$$
Also
$$Aw_n - (r_n + b_1) = b_n + r_n - (r_n + b_1) = b_n - b_1 \geq 0 \quad \forall n \geq n^*$$
wegen (5.26) und (5.40). Aus (5.41) folgt nun
$$Aw_n > 0 \quad \forall n \geq n^*$$

□

Bemerkungen:

1. In *Ho & Kashyap* [27] wird im Falle, daß das System $Aw > 0$ lösbar ist, wie folgt argumentiert:

Da aus Lemmata 5.7(2), 5.8, sowie aus dem Beweis von Lemma 5.9(1)

$$\Delta V(r_n) = \begin{cases} 0 & : \text{ falls } \ r_n = 0 \\ < 0 & : \text{ falls } \ r_n \neq 0 \end{cases} \tag{5.42}$$

kann man das Stabilitätskriterium für diskrete Systeme von Lyapunov anwenden, um daraus zu schließen, daß es

$$\lim_{n \to \infty} \|r_n\|_2^2 = 0$$

gelten muß. Doch Satz 5.7 kann nur dann angewandt werden, wenn (5.32) strikt *für alle* $u \neq v$ in einer Umgebung von $v = 0$ gültig ist und nicht nur für $u = r_n$, wie (5.42) versichert. Die Argumentation ist daher unklar, obwohl das Resultat immer noch stimmt.

2. In *Ho & Kashyap* [27] wird ohne Beweis behauptet, daß, falls $\Delta V(r_n) < 0$

$$\Delta V(r_n) \leq -\lambda(n)\|r_n\|_2^2 = -\lambda(n)V(r_n)$$

gelten muß, mit $\lambda(n) > 0$ den kleinsten positiven Eigenwert von $C_n^{\mathsf{T}}(\varrho^2 AA^+ + \varrho(1-\varrho)I)C_n$. Ist diese Behauptung richtig, so kann man weiter wie folgt argumentieren: Da es nur eine endliche Anzahl von Möglichkeiten gibt, die Matrix C_n zu bilden kann man

$$\lambda_* := \min_{n \in \mathbb{N}} \lambda(n)$$

definieren und es gilt $\lambda_* > 0$. Es folgt

$$\forall n \in \mathbb{N} : \Delta V(r_n) \leq -\lambda_* V(r_n)$$
$$\Leftrightarrow \forall n \in \mathbb{N} \quad \|r_{n+1}\|_2^2 - \|r_n\|_2^2 \leq -\lambda_* \|r_n\|_2^2$$
$$\Leftrightarrow \forall n \in \mathbb{N} \quad \|r_{n+1}\|_2^2 \leq (1 - \lambda_*)\|r_n\|_2^2 \tag{5.43}$$

Sei nun

$$r_{n+} \neq 0 \quad \forall n \in \mathbb{N}$$

Daher

$$r_n \neq 0 \quad \forall n \in \mathbb{N}$$

und es folgt

$$0 < \lambda_* < 1 \tag{5.44}$$

Durch Induktion erhält man aus (5.43)

$$\forall n \in \mathbb{N} \quad 0 < \|r_{n+1}\|_2^2 \leq (1 - \lambda_*)^n \|r_1\|_2^2 \tag{5.45}$$

Aus (5.44) folgt

$$\lim_{n\to\infty}(1-\lambda_*)^n\|r_1\|_2^2 = 0 \tag{5.46}$$

und aus (5.45), (5.46)

$$\lim_{n\to\infty}\|r_{n+1}\|_2^2 = 0 \Rightarrow \lim_{n\to\infty} r_n = 0 \tag{5.47}$$

Dies zusammen mit Lemma 5.12 hätte zur Folge, daß der Fall

$$r_{n+} \neq 0 \quad \forall n \in \mathbb{N}$$

nur bei lösbaren Systemen auftreten kann. Man findet tatsächlich diese Behauptung in *Ho & Kashyap* [27] und *Young & Calvert* [81] S. 135, allerdings ohne die obige Argumentation, sondern nur mit der Begründung, daß

$$\forall n \in \mathbb{N} : \Delta V(r_n) \leq 0, \quad V(r_n) \neq 0$$

3. In *Sklansky & Wassel* [69] S. 70, *Duda & Hart* [16] S. 163 wird dasselbe wie in Lemma 5.11 behauptet, doch ohne detaillierten Beweis.

Folgender Satz faßt alle Ergebnisse über das Verhalten des Ho-Kashyap-Algorithmus zusammen:

Satz 5.8 *Gegeben sei das lineare Ungleichungssystem*

$$Aw > 0$$

Für den Ho-Kashyap-Algorithmus 5.3 gilt

1. *Falls $Aw > 0$ lösbar ist, dann*

   (a) entweder
   $$\exists n^* \in \mathbb{N} : r_{n^*} = 0$$
   und $\{w_n, b_n\}_{n\in\mathbb{N}}$ wird stationär für $n \geq n^*$

   (b) oder $\lim_{n\to\infty} r_n = 0$ und
   $$\exists n^* \in \mathbb{N} : Aw_n > 0 \quad \forall n \geq n^*$$

2. *Falls $Aw > 0$ unlösbar ist, dann*

   $$r_n \neq 0 \quad \forall n \in \mathbb{N}$$

   und entweder

   $$\exists n^* \in \mathbb{N} : r_{n^*+} = 0 \quad und \quad \{w_n, b_n\}_{n\in\mathbb{N}} \quad wird \; stationär \; für \quad n \geq n^*$$

   oder

   $$\lim_{n\to\infty} r_{n+} = 0$$

In beiden Fällen gilt

$$r_n \neq 0 \Rightarrow r_n \not\geq 0$$
$$\exists \lambda > 0 : \Delta V(r_n) \leq -\lambda \|r_{n+}\|_2^2$$

wobei

$$V(r_n) := \|r_n\|_2^2$$
$$\Delta V(r_n) := V(r_{n+1}) - V(r_n)$$

$\square$

Beweis :

1. Das System $Aw > 0$ sei lösbar. Nach Lemma 5.7 gibt es zwei Möglichkeiten:

   (a)
   $$\exists n^* \in \mathbb{N} : r_{n^*} = 0$$

   Dann ist $r_{n^*+} = 0$ und aus (5.26) folgt, daß $\{w_n, b_n\}_{n \in \mathbb{N}}$ stationär für $n \geq n^*$ wird.

   (b)
   $$\forall n \in \mathbb{N} : r_{n+} \neq 0$$

   In diesem Fall gilt nach Lemma 5.11b)
   $$\lim_{n \to \infty} r_n = 0$$

   und nach Lemma 5.12
   $$\exists n^* \in \mathbb{N} : Aw_n > 0 \quad \forall n \geq n^*$$

2. Das System $Aw > 0$ sei unlösbar. Es folgt
   $$r_n \neq 0 \quad \forall n \in \mathbb{N}$$

   Aus Lemma 5.11 (1) folgt, daß entweder
   $$\exists n^* \in \mathbb{N} : r_{n^*+} = 0$$

   (und aus (5.26) folgt dann, daß $\{w_n, b_n\}_{n \in \mathbb{N}}$ stationär für $n \geq n^*$ wird) oder
   $$\lim_{n \to \infty} r_{n+} = 0, \quad r_{n+} \neq 0, \quad \forall n \in \mathbb{N}$$

Der Rest des Satzes folgt direkt aus Lemmata 5.7, und 5.10.

$\square$

Bemerkungen : Obiger Satz besagt folgendes:

1. Falls das System lösbar ist, dann erreicht der Algorithmus immer nach endlich vielen Schritten n^* eine Lösung w_{n^*}. Für sie gilt

    (a) entweder $Aw_{n^*} = b_{n^*} > 0$

    (b) oder $Aw_{n^*} \neq b_{n^*}$ aber trotzdem $Aw_{n^*} > 0$.

2. Falls das System unlösbar ist, dann entweder tritt nach endlich vielen Schritten $r_{n^*+} = 0$ ein, oder es gilt

$$\lim_{n \to \infty} r_{n+} = 0, \quad r_{n+} \neq 0, \quad \forall n \in \mathbb{N}$$

3. Falls $r_{n^*+} = 0$ und $Aw_{n^*} \not> 0$ für ein n^*, dann ist das System unlösbar. Somit hat man eine Abbruchbedingung.

4. Für beide Fälle gilt übrigens, daß nicht alle Komponenten von r_n positiv sein können und daß die Konvergenz gegen 0 für r_n bzw. r_{n+} wegen Lemma 5.10 schnell verläuft.

5. Falls $\{w_n\}_{n \in \mathbb{N}}$ konvergiert, hat man eine Lernregel im Sinne von Def. 3.1, die *Ho-Kashyap-Lernregel*. Die Abbruchbedingung und die schnelle Konvergenz machen die Ho-Kashyap-Lernregel theoretisch attraktiv.

Für eine einheitliche Formulierung der Perceptron-, Relaxations- und Ho-Kashyap-Lernregel s. *Ho & Kashyap* [28].

5.4   Methoden der linearen Programmierung

In diesem Abschnitt wird das System

$$Aw > 0 \tag{5.48}$$

in einem Problem der linearen Optimierung umgewandelt. Nachdem dies geschehen ist, kann man die Methoden der Linearen Programmierung z.B. den Simplex-Algorithmus anwenden, um das System zu lösen. Nach Lemma 5.2 kann man anstelle von (5.48) folgendes System betrachten

$$Aw - b \geq 0 \quad b > 0 \quad \text{beliebig} \tag{5.49}$$

Im folgenden werden zwei verschiedene Formulierungen von (5.49) als LP-Problem dargestellt:

1. Formulierung : (s. *Duda & Hart* [16] S. 166)

Man führe die künstliche Variable $t \in \mathbb{R}$ ein und betrachte das System

$$
\begin{aligned}
Aw - b + t(1, \ldots, 1)^\top &\geq 0 \\
t &\geq 0
\end{aligned}
\tag{5.50}
$$

Man beachte, daß $w = 0, t = \max_i b_i$ eine Lösung (eine sog. zullassige Basislösung) von (5.50) ist (i steht für die i-te Koordinate). Eine Lösung (w, t) mit $t = 0$ von (5.50) ist zugleich Lösung von (5.48). Falls t nicht Null sein kann, ist (5.48) unlösbar. Dadurch gelangt man zu folgendem LP-Problem: Man minimiere t über alle t und w, die (5.50) erfüllen. Da w eine freie Variable ist, spaltet man sie auf:

$$w = w^+ - w^-$$

mit

$$w^+ = \frac{1}{2}(|w| + w)$$
$$w^- = \frac{1}{2}(|w| - w)$$

Somit erhält man die Standardformulierung:

$$\text{Minimiere } z := c^\top u$$
unter den Nebenbedingungen:

$$
\begin{aligned}
A'u &\geq b \\
u &\geq 0
\end{aligned}
$$
(5.51)

mit

$$
\begin{aligned}
A' &:= (A \quad -A \quad e) \\
u &:= (w^+ \quad w^- \quad t)^\top \\
c &:= (0 \quad 0 \quad 1)^\top \\
e &:= (1, \ldots, 1)^\top \\
b &= \text{beliebig, mit} \quad b > 0
\end{aligned}
$$

2. Formulierung : (s. *Smith* [70])

Man versuche

$$J(w) := \sum_{a_{i_n} \in \Psi(w)} (b_{i_n} - a_{i_n}^\top w)$$

zu minimieren, wobei $a_i^\top$ die i-te Zeile von A und

$$\Psi(w) := \{a_i / a_i^\top w - b_i < 0\}$$

die Menge der von w falsch klassifizierten a_i. Leider ist $J(w)$ keine lineare, sondern eine stückweise lineare Funktion von w. Trotzdem kann man ein LP-Problem formulieren und zwar wie folgt :

Man führe den Vektor

$$t := (t_1, \ldots, t_p)^\top$$

ein und versuche

$$z := \sum_{i=1}^p t_i \tag{5.52}$$

unter den Nebenbedingungen

$$
\begin{aligned}
t &\geq 0 \\
Aw - b + t &\geq 0
\end{aligned}
\tag{5.53}
$$

zu minimieren. Für jedes w ist der Minimum-Wert von z gleich $J(w)$, denn unter den Bed. (5.53) ist der beste Vektor $t = \max(0, b - Aw)$, wobei $\max(\cdot)$ komponentenweise angewandt wird. Daher erreicht $J(w)$ genau dann sein Minimum, wenn z von (5.52) unter (5.53) sein Minimum erreicht. Somit erhält man die Standardformulierung:

Minimiere $z := c^\top u$
unter den Nebenbedingungen:

$$
\begin{aligned}
A'u &\geq b \\
u &\geq 0
\end{aligned}
\tag{5.54}
$$

mit

$$
\begin{aligned}
A' &:= (A \quad -A \quad I_p) \\
u &:= (w^+ \quad w^- \quad t)^\top \\
c &:= (0 \quad 0 \quad e_p)^\top \\
e_p &:= \underbrace{(1, \ldots, 1)}_{p\text{-Mal}}{}^\top \\
b &= \text{beliebig, mit } \ b > 0
\end{aligned}
$$

Eine zulässige Basislösung von (5.54) ist $(w, t) = (0, b)$. Man kann somit den Simplex-Algorithmus initialisieren, der in endlich vielen Schritten ein w erreichen wird, daß $J(w)$ minimiert. Man beachte, daß, dank der Wahl von $J(w)$, das minimierende w_* auch dann sinnvoll ist, wenn $J(w_*) \neq 0$: $J(w)$ ist ein intuitiv sinnvoller Fehlermaß.

Es gibt auch andere Formulierungen von (5.48) als LP-Problem (s. *Grinold* [20], *Mangasarian* [46], *Highleyman* [26]). Der interessierte Leser sei auf die Originalliteratur verwiesen.

Kapitel 6

Computer-Simulation

Die in Kapitel 5 vorgestellten Methoden wurden in einer Computer-Simulation getestet. Im folgenden werden die Durchführung und Implementierung beschrieben und die theoretischen Erwartungen den Simulations-Ergebnissen gegenübergestellt. Für relevanten Studien siehe *Mays* [48] (nur binäre Vektoren), *Shavlik et al* [67] (Vergleich mit symbolischen Algorithmen).

6.1 Durchführung

1. Mittels eines Zufallsgenerators wurde ein Vektor $w_* \in [-1,+1]^n$ konstruiert. Für seine Koordinaten wurde die gleichmäßige Verteilung im $[-1,+1]$ zugrundegelegt.

2. Mit der Methode von 1) wurden weitere Vektoren a_j konstruiert. Die ersten m davon, für welche $w_*^\top a_j > 0$ galt, wurden als die m Zeilen der Matrix $A \in \mathbb{R}^{m \times n}$ akzeptiert.

3. Es galt, eine Lösung w zu $Aw > 0$ mittels der verschiedenen Methoden zu berechnen. Das System ist lösbar, da nach Konstruktion $Aw_* > 0$.

4. Die Perceptron- , Relaxations- , Ho-Kashyap- und Simplex-Methoden wurden eingesetzt. Die Zeit, die jede Methode benötigte, um zu einer Lösung zu gelangen, wurde gemessen.

5. Das obige Schema wurde 10 Mal durchgeführt, jeweils mit verschiedenen Zufallsvektoren. Von den gemessenen Zeiten wurden Mittelwert und Standard-Abweichung berechnet.

6. Das ganze wurde für $n = 5, 10, 15, \ldots, 80$ und $m = 5, 10, 15, \ldots, 265$ wiederholt.

Die einzelnen Methoden wurden wie folgt eingesetzt:

- **Perceptron-Lernregel:** Es wurde der Algorithmus (5.2) mit $w_1 = 0$ eingesetzt.

- **Relaxations-Lernregel:** Es wurde der Algorithmus (5.15) mit $w_1 = 0$, $\lambda = 2$ eingesetzt.

- **Ho-Kashyap-Lernregel:** Es wurde der Algorithmus (5.26) mit $\varrho = 0.9$, $b_1 = (1, \ldots, 1)^\mathsf{T}$ eingesetzt.

- **Simplex-Methoden:** Die zwei in Kap. 5 besprochenen Methoden werden mit *Simplex 1* bzw. *Simplex 2* bezeichnet.

  1. **Simplex 1:** Äquivalent zur Standard-Formulierung (5.51) wurde folgendes Problem gelöst:

$$\text{Minimiere } c^\mathsf{T} u \text{ mit}$$

$$\begin{aligned} u &= (w, t)^\mathsf{T} \quad t \in \mathrm{R} \\ c &= (0, 1)^\mathsf{T} \end{aligned}$$

unter den Nebenbedingungen

$$\begin{aligned} (-\infty, 0)^\mathsf{T} &\leq (w, t)^\mathsf{T} \leq (+\infty, +\infty)^\mathsf{T} \\ (1, \ldots, 1)^\mathsf{T} = b &\leq (A \quad e)u \leq (+\infty, \ldots, +\infty)^\mathsf{T} \end{aligned} \quad (6.1)$$

wobei $e = (1, \ldots, 1)^\mathsf{T}$. Als Anfangsvektor wurde $(0, \max_{i=1,\ldots,m}\{b_i\}) = (0, 1)$ benutzt.

  2. **Simplex 2:** Äquivalent zur Standard-Formulierung (5.54) wurde folgendes Problem gelöst:

$$\text{Minimiere } c^\mathsf{T} u \text{ mit}$$

$$\begin{aligned} u &= (w, t)^\mathsf{T} \quad t \in \mathrm{R}^m \\ c &= (0, e_m)^\mathsf{T} \\ e_m &= \underbrace{(1, \ldots, 1)}_{m\text{-Mal}}^\mathsf{T} \end{aligned}$$

unter den Nebenbedingungen

$$\begin{aligned} (-\infty, 0)^\mathsf{T} &\leq (w, t)^\mathsf{T} \leq (+\infty, +\infty)^\mathsf{T} \\ (1, \ldots, 1)^\mathsf{T} = b &\leq (A \quad I_m)u \leq (+\infty, \ldots, +\infty)^\mathsf{T} \end{aligned} \quad (6.2)$$

Als Anfangsvektor wurde $(0, b)$ benutzt.

Die Formulierungen (6.1) und (6.2) waren durch die verwendete Bibliothek-Routine bedingt.

6.2 Implementierung

Das Simulationsprogram wurde in FORTRAN geschrieben und auf dem SIEMENS 7.590-R-Großrechner des Rechenzentrums der Universität Kaiserslautern durchgeführt. Zur Lösung der einzelnen mathematischen Probleme wurden folgende Routinen der NAG-Bibliothek [53] eingesetzt:

- **G05CCF, G05FAF:** Zur Erzeugung von Zufallszahlen.

- **F01BLF** : Zur Berechnung der Moore-Penrose-Inverse einer Matrix für die Ho-Kashyap-Methode.

- **E04MBF** : Zur Lösung eines LP-Problems.

- **F06-Routinen** : Zur Durchführung von Vektor- und Matrix-Vektor- Operationen.

- **G01AAF** : Zu Statistik-Berechnungen.

Im Anhang A befindet sich ein Ausdruck des Quell-Programms. Die darin enthaltene Kommentare sollten ausreichen, um dem interessierten Leser einen klaren Eindruck über den Programmablauf zu vermitteln. Das Programm wurde für Fehlerfreiheit mehrfach getestet. Im Anhang B befindet sich ein Ausdruck eines solches Probelaufs.

Folgende Besonderheiten waren implementierungsbedingt:

- **F01BLF** : Diese Routine berechnet die Moore-Penrose-Inverse A^+ einer Matrix $A \in \mathbb{R}^{m \times n}$ nur im Fall $m \geq n$. Falls $m < n$ muß man $(A^\top)^+$ berechnen und das Ergebnis transponieren. Ferner hängt der Erfolg der Berechnung vom Wert des Toleranz-Parameters TOL. Falls TOL zu groß bzw. zu klein ist, bricht F01BLF ab und signalisiert das Problem durch den Wert des IFAIL-Parameters. Diese Information wird vom Programm genutzt, um den Wert von TOL nach unten bzw. oben zu ändern. Danach wird F01BLF wieder aufgerufen. Dies hat gegebenfalls störende Auswirkungen auf das zeitliche Verhalten des Verfahrens.

- **E04MBF** : Bei Simplex 1 und $n = 30$ bricht diese Routine für $m > 180$ ab. Bei größerem n wird die Abbruchgrenze für m noch kleiner. Als Grund des Abbruchs gibt die Routine folgendes an:

    'Insgesamt 50 Änderungen wurden am Arbeitssatz vorgenommen, ohne den Wert von x zu ändern. Es findet wahrscheinlich zyklische Vertauschung statt. Der Benutzer sollte die Möglichkeit in Betracht ziehen, die routine E04NAF mit MSGLVL=5 zu benutzen, um die Einführung und Eliminierung von Nebenbedingungen zu überwachen und eine eventuelle zyklische Vertauschung aufzuspüren'.

Um die Testbedingungen bei allen Methoden gleich zu halten wurde auf den empfohlenen Benutzer-Eingriff verzichtet. Daher wurden alle Methoden für jedes n nur bis zum letzten Wert von m getestet, der frei von solchen Abbrüchen war.

6.3   Theoretisches Verhalten

Aus den Implementierungsbedingungen und den theoretischen Ergebnißen vom Kap. 5 lassen sich für das zeitliche Verhalten der Methoden einige Schlüße ziehen:

6.3.1   Perceptron-Lernregel

Nach Satz (5.3) gilt für die maximale Anzahl von Iterationen n_0 :

$$n_0 \leq \left[\frac{\|w_1 - \overline{w}\|_2^2}{\beta^2} \right] + 1 \tag{6.3}$$

mit

$$
\begin{aligned}
\alpha &= \inf_{n \in \mathbb{N}} \{\varrho_n\} \min_{j \in \{1,\dots,m\}} \{w_*^\mathsf{T} a_j\} \\
\beta &= \sup_{n \in \mathbb{N}} \{\varrho_n\} \max_{j \in \{1,\dots,m\}} \{\|a_j\|_2\} \\
w_* &: \quad \text{eine Lösung von} \quad Aw > 0 \\
\overline{w} &= \frac{\beta^2}{\alpha} w_*
\end{aligned}
$$

Für die durchgeführte Simulation gilt

$$
\begin{aligned}
w_1 &= 0 \\
a_j, w_* &\in [-1, +1]^n \quad \forall j = 1, \dots, m \\
\varrho_n &= 1 \quad \forall n \in \mathbb{N}
\end{aligned} \tag{6.4}
$$

Daher

$$
\begin{aligned}
\|a_j\|_2 &\leq \sqrt{n} \quad \forall j \in \{1, \dots, m\} \\
\|w_*\|_2 &\leq \sqrt{n} \\
\beta &\leq \sqrt{n}
\end{aligned}
$$

und aus (6.3) mit der Vereinfachung, daß Gauß-Klammer und Einheit nicht berücksichtigt werden (dabei ist der maximale Fehler gleich 1)

$$n_0 \leq \frac{\|\overline{w}\|_2^2}{\beta^2} = \frac{\frac{\beta^4}{\alpha^2} \|w_*\|_2^2}{\beta^2} = \frac{\beta^2}{\alpha^2} \|w_*\|_2^2 \leq \frac{n^2}{\alpha^2}$$

Aus der Implementierung (s. Programm im Anhang A) ergibt sich, daß für jede Iteration maximal mn Multiplikationen durchgeführt werden müssen (Additionen, Indexierungen und Zuweisungsanweisungen wurden nicht berücksichtigt). Man erhält somit eine Schranke für die benötigte Zeit

$$T \leq \frac{n^3 m t_{mult}}{\alpha^2}$$

wobei t_{mult} die CPU-Zeit für eine Multiplikation ist. Der Wert von α ist von m und n abhängig. Auf eine statistische Berechnung seines Mittelwertes wird hier verzichtet. T ist also im schlimmsten Fall eine Funktion von m und n der Form

$$T = t_{mult} \frac{mn^3}{\alpha^2(m,n)} \tag{6.5}$$

6.3.2 Relaxations-Lernregel

Nach Satz (5.6) und Lemma 5.3 gilt für die maximale Anzahl von Iterationen n_0 :

$$n_0 \; < \; \frac{\|w_1 - \overline{w}\|_2^2}{\beta^2} + 1$$

mit :

$$\overline{w} \; = \; \frac{\lambda e_2(\|w_1 - \frac{d}{\alpha}w_*\|_2 + \frac{d}{\alpha}\|w_*\|_2 + \frac{d}{e_1}) + d}{\alpha} w_*$$

w_* : eine Lösung von $\quad Aw > 0$

$$d \; = \; \max_{i\in\{1,\dots,m\}}\{b_i\}$$

$$\alpha \; = \; \min_{i\in\{1,\dots,m\}}\{(Aw_*)_i\} = \min_{i\in\{1,\dots,m\}}\{a_i^\top w_*\}$$

a_i : i-te Spalte von $\quad A^\top$

$$e_1 \; = \; \min_{i\in\{1,\dots,m\}}\{\|a_i\|_2\}$$

$$e_2 \; = \; \max_{i\in\{1,\dots,m\}}\{\|a_i\|_2\}$$

$$c_1 \; = \; \varrho_{min}$$

$$c_2 \; = \; \varrho_{max}$$

$$\beta \; = \; \sqrt{c_1 c_2} \tag{6.6}$$

Für die durchgeführte Simulation gilt

$$\begin{aligned} w_1 &= 0 \\ b &= (1,\dots,1)^\top \\ \lambda &= 2 \\ a_j, w_* &\in [-1,+1]^n \quad \forall j = 1,\dots,m \end{aligned} \tag{6.7}$$
$$\tag{6.8}$$

Daher

$$\begin{aligned} \|a_j\|_2 &\le \sqrt{n} \quad \forall j \in \{1,\dots,m\} \\ e_2 &\le \sqrt{n} \\ \|w_*\|_2 &\le \sqrt{n} \\ d &= 1 \end{aligned} \tag{6.9}$$

Es folgt

$$\|\overline{w}\|_2 \leq \frac{2\sqrt{n}(2\frac{1}{\alpha}\sqrt{n} + \frac{1}{e_1}) + 1}{\alpha}\sqrt{n} = \frac{4n\sqrt{n}}{\alpha^2} + \frac{2n}{\alpha e_1} + \frac{\sqrt{n}}{\alpha}$$

$$n_0 < \frac{\|w\|_2^2}{\beta^2} + 1$$

Der Näherungs-Ansatz von maximal mn Multiplikationen per Iteration gilt auch hier und somit erhält man eine Schranke für die benötigte Zeit

$$T < t_{mult} \left\{ \frac{\left(\frac{4n\sqrt{n}}{\alpha^2} + \frac{2n}{\alpha e_1} + \frac{\sqrt{n}}{\alpha}\right)^2}{\beta^2} + 1 \right\} mn$$

wobei t_{mult} die CPU-Zeit für eine Multiplikation ist. Die Werte von α, e_1 sind von m und n abhängig. Auf deren statistische Untersuchung wird verzichtet. Eine konkrete Abschätzung für β scheint schwierig zu sein.

6.3.3   Ho-Kashyap-Lernregel

Wegen der schnellen Konvergenz der Ho-Kashyap-Lernregel liegt der Verdacht nahe, daß ein großer Teil der benötigten Zeit für die Berechnung der Moore-Penrose-Inverse aufgebracht wird. Nach dem NAG-Handbuch [53] ist die F01BLF-Zeit analog zu $mn\text{Rang}(A)$. Da immer $m \geq n$ sein muß, ergibt sich für Matrizen A maximalen Ranges (s. Abschnitt 6.2)

$$\text{F01BLF-Zeit} \leq \begin{cases} c_1 n m^2 & : \quad m < n \\ c_2 m n^2 & : \quad \text{sonst} \end{cases}$$

mit geeigneten Konstanten $c_1, c_2 > 0$. Falls also die Berechnung der Moore-Penrose-Inverse einen dominanten Zeitanteil in Anspruch nimmt, kann man für festes $n = n_0$ eine Änderung des zeitlichen Verhaltens bei $m = n_0$ von höherer auf niedrigere Ordnung bzgl. m erwarten.

Überdurchschnittliche Schwankungen der Zeit sind zu erwarten, falls der TOL-Parameter zu groß bzw. zu klein gewählt wurde: dann wird nämlich automatisch eine Versuchs- und Irrtums-Schleife eingeschaltet, die, bis sie zu einem akzeptablen TOL-Wert einpendelt, die Rechenzeit belastet.

6.3.4   Simplex-Methoden

Nach dem NAG-Handbuch [53] ist die Zeit für eine Iteration der E04MBF-Routine analog zu $\min(N^2, NCLIN^2)$. Dabei ist N die Dimension des unbekannten Vektors u (s. Abschnitt 6.1) und $NCLIN$ die Anzahl der linearen Nebenbedingungen. Für

Simplex 1 ist $N = n+1$, $NCLIN = m$ und für Simplex 2 $N = m+n$, $NCLIN = m$. Daher gilt für die Iterationszeit T_{Iter}

$$T_{Iter} = \begin{cases} cm^2 & : & m \leq n+1 \\ c'(n+1)^2 & : & \text{sonst} \end{cases}$$

für Simplex 1 und

$$T_{Iter} = c''m^2$$

für Simplex 2 ($c, c', c'' > 0$ geeignete Konstanten). Für die gesamte Zeit T erhält man

$$T = \begin{cases} cm^2 I(m,n) & : & m \leq n+1 \\ c'(n+1)^2 I(m,n) & : & \text{sonst} \end{cases}$$

für Simplex 1 und

$$T = c''m^2 I(m,n)$$

für Simplex 2. $I(m,n)$ bezeichnet die benötigte Anzahl von Iterationen. Folglich ist eine qualitative Änderung im zeitlichen Verhalten der Simplex 1 für festes n an der Stelle $m = n+1$ zu erwarten.

6.4 Simulationsergebnisse

Die Ergebnisse der Simulation sind im Anhang C zu sehen. Für festes n wurden jeweils die Mittelwerte der gemessenen Zeiten für variables m gezeichnet. Die Zeichnungsgrenzen sind bei allen Zeichnungen die selben. Da teilweise große Zeitunterschiede unter den getesteten Methoden gemessen wurden, wurde die Wahl der Zeichnungsgrenzen durch Kompromiße bestimmt. So blieb ein Teil der Simplex-2-Kurve stets außerhalb der Zeichnung. Dasselbe gilt für manche stark oszillierende Teile der Ho-Kashyap-Kurve. Trotz dieser Unannehmlichkeiten sind folgende Ergebnisse klar feststellbar:

- Die Simplex-2-Methode dauert am längsten.

- Dagegen ist die Simplex-1-Methode für $n \leq 20$ entweder die beste (vor allem für großes $m : m \geq 150$) oder unter den besten.

- Die Perceptron- und Relaxations-Lernregeln weisen ziemlich dasselbe zeitliche Verhalten auf. Ab etwa $n = 20$ liefern sie die schnellsten Zeiten. Ihre Kurven sind meistens sehr nah aneinander. Ihre Steigung bzgl. m ist sehr mild.

- Bei der Ho-Kashyap-Lernregel bekommt man ab etwa $m = 140$ Schwierigkeiten mit dem TOL-Parameter. Dies führt zu starken Schwankungen der Zeiten.

- Ab ewa $n = 20$ sind die schnellsten Methoden der Reihe nach zuerst die Perceptron- und die Relaxations-Lernregeln gefolgt von den Ho-Kashyap-, Simplex-1- und Simplex-2-Methoden. Dies bleibt so — es wird sogar verstärkt — bis $n = 80$.

- Ab $n = 45$ ist bei der Ho-Kashyap-Kurve bei $n = n_0$ (= aktueller n-Wert) eine qualitative Änderung vom deutlich nicht-linearem zum milderen Verhalten sichtbar.

- Ein ähnlicher 'Knick' ist ab $n = 60$ bei der Simplex-1-Kurve klar zu erkennen.

Die obigen Ergebnisse und das allgemeine qualitative Verhalten der Kurven unterstützen die theoretischen Überlegungen des letzten Abschnittes.

Nicht zu sehen in den Zeichnungen sind die Standard-Abweichungen. Im Bereich der starken Schwankungen sind sie erwartungsgemäß für die Ho-Kashyap-Zeiten besonders groß. Bis etwa $n = 20$ sind sie aber auch für die Perceptron- und Relaxations-Lernregeln sehr groß: teilweise so groß, wie die Mittelwerte selbst. Dies ist bei der Beurteilung der Methoden zu beachten.

Unter den genannten Methoden gab es keinen eindeutigen Testsieger. Vielmehr ist die Wahl der geeignetesten Methode unter folgenden Kriterien zu treffen:

- Zeitliches Verhalten bzgl. m und n.

- Erkennung eines unlösbaren Systems.

- Sinnvolle Lösung auch im unlösbaren Fall.

- Toleranz gegen Eingabefehler.

- Serieller oder Parallel-Rechner.

- Speicherplatzbedarf.

- Einfachheit des Algorithmus.

- Hardware-Implementierbarkeit.

Diese Arbeit würde ihr Ziel erreichen, wenn sie dem potentiellen Anwender die Wahl bezüglich einiger dieser Kriterien erleichtern würde.

Literaturverzeichnis

[1] **Agmon, S** , *'The relaxation method for linear inequalities'* , Canad. J. Math. , Vol. 6 , **1954** , pp. 382–392

[2] **Albert, A A** , *'Regression and the Moore-Penrose pseudoinverse'* , Academic Press, **1972**

[3] **Amari, S-I** , *'Neural theory of association and concept formation'* , Biol. Cybern. Vol. 26 , **1977** , pp. 175–185

[4] **Amari, S-I** , *'Field theory of self-organizing neural nets'* , IEEE Trnas. SMC, Vol. SMC-13, **Sept./Oct. 1983** , pp. 741–748

[5] **Anderson, J A** , *'Two models for memory organization using interacting traces'*, Math. Biosci. , Vol. 8 , **1970** , pp. 137–160

[6] **Anderson, J A** , *'Cognitive and psychological computation with neural models'*, IEEE Trans. SMC, Vol. SMC-13, **Sept./Oct. 1983** , pp. 799–815

[7] **Barto, A G, Sutton, R S, Anderson, C W** , *'Neuronlike adaptive elements that can solve difficult learning control problems'*, IEEE Trans. SMC, Vol. SMC-13, **Sept./Oct. 1983** , pp. –

[8] **Baum, E B** , *'On the capabilities of multilayer perceptrons'* , Journal of Complexity, Vol. 4 , **1988** , pp. 193–215

[9] **Baum, E B, Haussler, D** , *'What size net gives valid generalization?'* , in **Touretzky, D (Ed.)** , *'Advances in neural information processing systems I'* , Morgann Kaufmann Publishers **1989** , pp. 81–90

[10] **Ben-Israel, A, Greville, T N E** , *'Generalized inverses: theory and applications'* , John Wiley & Sons, **1974**

[11] **Block, H D, Levin, S A** , *'On the boundedness of an iterative procedure for solving a system of linear inequalities'*, Proc. Amer. Math. Soc. , Vol. 26 , **Oct. 1970** , pp. 229–235

[12] **Blum, A, Rivest, R** , *'Training a 3-node neural network is NP-complete'* , in **Touretzky, D (Ed.)** , *'Advances in neural information processing systems I'* , Morgann Kaufmann Publishers **1989** , pp. 494–501

[13] **Cover, T M** , *'Geometrical and statistical properties of systems of linear inequalities with applications in pattern recognition'*,IEEE Trans. Elec. Comp. , Vol. EC-14,**1965** , pp. 326–334

[14] **Dines, L L** , *'Systems of linear inequalities'* , Ann. of Math. , Vol. 20 , **1919** , pp. 191–199

[15] **Duda, R O, Fossum, H** , *'Pattern classification by iteratively determined linear and piecewise linear discriminant functions'*, IEEE Trans. Elec. Comp. , Vol. EC-15,**April 1966** , pp. 220–232

[16] **Duda, R O, Hart, P E** , *'Pattern classification and scene analysis'* , John Wiley & Sons, New York, **1973**

[17] **Duffin, R J** , *" On Fourier's analysis of linear inequality systems"* , Mathematical Programming Study I, **1974** , pp. 71–95

[18] **Gelperin, A E, Hopfield, J J, Tank, D W** , *'The logic of* limax *learning'* , Model neural networks and behavior, New York, Plenum, **1985** , pp. 237–261

[19] **Golub, G H, Van Loan, C F** , *'Matrix computations'* , John Hopkins University Press, Baltimore, Maryland, **1983**

[20] **Grinold, R C** , *"Comment on 'Pattern classification design by linear programming'"*, IEEE Trans. on Comp. (Correspondence), Vol. C-18, **April 1969**, pp. 378–379

[21] **Grossberg, S** , *'Some networks that can learn, remember and reproduce any number of complicated, space-time patterns I'*, J. Math. & Mech. Vol. 19 , **1969**, pp. 53–91

[22] **Grossberg, S** , *'Some networks that can learn, remember and reproduce any number of complicated, space-time patterns II'*, Stud. App. Math. Vol. 49 , **1970**,- pp. 135–166

[23] **Grossberg, S** , *'Competitive learning: from interactive activation to adaptive reasoning'*, Cognitive Science, Vol. 11 , **1987** , pp. 23–63

[24] **Hebb, D O** , *'Organization of behavior'* , John Wiley & Sons, New York, **1949**

[25] **Hecht-Nielsen, R** , *'Neurocomputer applications'* , in **Eckmiller, R, Malsburg, C v d (Eds.)** , *Neural computers* , NATO ASI Series, Vol. F41 , Springer-Verlag ,**1988** , pp. 445–453

[26] **Highleyman, W H** , *'A note on linear separation'* , IEEE Trans. Elec. Comp., Vol. EC-10,**Dec. 1961** , pp. 777–778

[27] **Ho, Y C, Kashyap, R L** , *'An algorithm for linear inequalities and its applications'* , IEEE Trans. Elec. Comp. , Vol. EC-14,**Oct. 1965** , pp. 683–688

[28] **Ho, Y C, Kashyap, R L** , *'A class of iterative procedures for linear inequalities'*, J. SIAM Control, Vol. 4 , **1966** , pp. 112–115

[29] **Hopfield, J J**, *'Neural networks and physical systems with emergent collective computational abilities*, Proc.Nat.Acad.Sci.USA, Vol. 79, **April 1982**, pp. 2554-2558

[30] **Hopfield, J J**, *'Neurons with graded responce have collective computational properties like those of two-state neurons'*, Proc.Nat.Acad.Sci.USA, Vol. 81, **May 1984**, pp. 3088-3092

[31] **Hopfield, J J, Tank, D W**, *'Neural computations of decisions on optimization problems'*, Biol. Cybern., Vol. 52, No. 3, **1985**, pp. 141-152

[32] **Houle, M E**, *'Theorems on the existence of separating surfaces'*, Discrete Comput. Geom., Vol. 6, **1991**, pp. 49-56

[33] **Judd, S**, *'Learning in networks is hard'*, IEEE 1st Int. Conf. Neural Networks, San Diego CA, June 21-24, Vol. II, **1987**, pp. 685-692

[34] **Karna, K N, Breen, D M**, *'An artificial neural networks tutorial: part 1 — basics'*, Neural Networks, Vol. 1, **Jan. 1989**, pp. 4-23

[35] **Kelley, W G, Peterson, A C**, *'Difference equations: An introduction with applications'*, Academic Press, **1991**

[36] **Kirchberger, P**, *'Über Tchebychefsche Annäherungsmethoden'*, Math. Ann., Vol. 57, **1903**, pp. 509-540

[37] **Knobloch, H W, Kwakernaak, H**, *'Lineare Kontrolltheorie'*, Springer-Verlag, Berlin-Heidelberg-New York-Tokio, **1985**

[38] **Kohonen, T, Oja, E, Ruohonen, M**, *'Adaptation of a linear system to a finite set of patterns occurring in an arbitrarily varying order'*, Acta Polytecnica Scandinavica, Mathematics and computing machinery series, No. 25, **1974**

[39] **Kohonen, T, Reuhkala, E, Mäkisara, K, Vainio, L**, *'Associative recall of images'*, Biol. Cybern., Vol. 22, **1976**, pp. 159-168

[40] **Kohonen, T**, *'Associative memory — a system theoretical approach'*, Springer-Verlag, **1978**

[41] **Kolmogorov, A N, Fomin, S V**, *'Introductory real analysis'*, Prentice-Hall, **1970**

[42] **Kosko, B**, *'Constructing an associative memory'*, BYTE, **Sept. 1987**, pp. 137-144

[43] **Kuhn, H W**, *'Solvability and consistency for linear equations and inequalities'*, Amer. Math. Monthly, Vol. 63, **1956**, pp. 217-232

[44] **Lin, J H, Vitter, S J**, *'Complexity results on learning by neural nets'*, Machine Learning, Vol. 6, **1991**, pp. 211-230

[45] **Lippmann, R P** , *'An introduction to computing with neural nets'* , IEEE ASSP Magazine, *April 1987* , pp 4–22

[46] **Mangasarian, O L** , *'Linear and non-linear separation of patterns by linear programming'*, Operations Research, Vol. 13 , **May/June 1965**, pp. 444–452

[47] **Mangasarian, O L** , *'Multisurface methods of pattern separation'*, IEEE Trans. Info. Theory, Vol. IT-14,**Nov. 1968** , pp. 801–807

[48] **Mays, C H** , *'Effects of adaptation parameters on convergence time and tolerance for adaptive threshold elements'*, IEEE Trans. Elec. Comp. , Vol. EC-13,**Aug. 1964** , pp. 465–468

[49] **McCulloch, W S, Pitts, W H** , *'A logical calculus of the ideas immanent in nervous activity'* , Bulletin of Math. Biophysics, Vol. 5 , **1943** , pp. 115–133

[50] **Meisel, W S** , *'Computer-oriented approaches to pattern recognition'* , Academic Press, **1972**

[51] **Minsky, M, Papert, S** , *'Perceptrons: An introduction to computational geometry'* , MIT Press, **1969**

[52] **Motzkin, T S, Schoenberg, J** , *'The relaxation method for linear inequalities'*, Canad. J. Math. , Vol. 6 , **1954** , pp. 393–404

[53] **NAG Ltd** , *'NAG Fortran library manual, Mark 14'* , Oxford, **April 1990**

[54] **Obermeier, K K, Barron, J J** , *'Time to get fired up'* , BYTE, **Aug. 1989**, pp. 217–224

[55] **Palm, G** , *'On representation and approximation of non-linear systems'* , Biol. Cybern. , Vol. 31 , **1978** , pp. 119–124

[56] **Palm, G** , *'On representation and approximation of non-linear systems II'* , Biol. Cybern. , Vol. 34 , **1979** , pp. 49–52

[57] **Palm, G** , *'On associative memory'* , Biol. Cybern. , Vol. 36 , **1980** , pp. 19–31

[58] **Penrose, R** , *'A generalized inverse for matrices'* , Proc. Cambridge Philos. Soc. , Vol. 51 , **1955** , pp. 406–413

[59] **Penrose, R** , *'On best approximate solutions of linear matrix equations'* , Proc. Cambridge Philos. Soc. , Vol. 52 , **1956** , pp. 17–19

[60] **Rao, C R, Mitra, S K** , *'Generalized inverse of matrices and its applications'*, John Wiley, New York, **1971**

[61] **Rescorla, R A, Wagner, A R** , *'A theory of Pavlovian conditioning: variations in the effectiveness of reinforcement and non-reinforcement'*, in **Black, A H, Prokasy, W F (Eds.)** , *'Classical conditioning II: current research and theory'* , Appleton-Crafts, **1972**

[62] **Richter, M M** , *'Konnektionismus'* , Vorlesungsskript, Universität Kaiserslautern, **1990**

[63] **Rosenblatt, F** , *'Principles of neurodynamics: perceptrons and the theory of brain mechanisms'*, Spartan Books, Washington, D.C. , **1962**

[64] **Rummelhart, D E, Hinton, G E, Mc Clelland, J L** , *'A general framework for parallel distributed processing'* , in Parallel distributed processing: Explorations in the microstructure of cognition , Vol. 1 (Rummelhart, Mc Clelland and the PDP Research Group), *MIT Press* , Cambridge MA, **1986**

[65] **Rummelhart, D E, Hinton, G E, Williams, R J** , *'Learning internal representations by error propagation'*, in Parallel distributed processing: Explorations in the microstructure of cognition , Vol. 1 (Rummelhart, Mc Clelland and the PDP Research Group), *MIT Press* , Cambridge MA, **1986**

[66] **Sejnowski, T J** , *'Neural network learning algorithms'* , in **Eckmiller, R, Malsburg, C v d (Eds.)** , *Neural computers* , NATO ASI Series, Vol. F41 , Springer-Verlag ,**1988** , pp. 291–299

[67] **Shavlik, W J, Mooney, R J, Towell, G G** , *'Symbolic and neural learning algorithms: an experimental comparison'*, Machine Learning, Vol. 6 , **1991** , pp. 111–143

[68] **Singleton, R C** , *'A test for linear separability as applied to self-organizing machines'* in **Yovits, M C et al. (Eds.)** , *Self Organizing Systems* , Spartan Books, Washington, D.C. , **1962** , pp. 503–524. Reprinted in **Sklansky, J (Ed.), Dowden, Hutchinson & Ross** , *'Pattern recognition'* , Stroutsburg, PA, **1973**, pp. 55–76

[69] **Sklansky, J, Wassel, N G** , *'Pattern classifiers and trainable machines'* , Springer-Verlag, New York-Heidelberg-Berlin, **1981**

[70] **Smith, F W** , *'Pattern classifier design by linear programming'* , IEEE Trans. on Comp. Vol. C-17, **April 1968** , pp. 367–372

[71] **Smith, F W** , *'Design of multicategory pattern classifiers with two-category classifier design procedures'*, IEEE Trans. on Comp. , Vol. C-18, **June 1969** , pp. 548–551

[72] **Steinbuch, K** , *'Die Lernmatrix'* , Kybernetik (Biol. Cybern.), Vol. 1 , **1961**, pp. 36–45

[73] **Steinbuch, K, Piske, U A W** , *'Learning matrices and their applications'* , IEEE Trans. Elec. Comp. , Vol. 12 , **Dec. 1963**

[74] **Stoer, J, Witzgall, C** , *'Convexity and optimization in finite dimensions I'* , Springer-Verlag, Berlin-Heidelberg-New York, **1970**

[75] **Stone, G O** , *'An analysis of the delta rule and the learning of statistical associations'* , in Parallel distributed processing: Explorations in the microstructure of cognition , Vol. 1 (Rummelhart, Mc Clelland and the PDP Research Group), Chapter 11, *MIT Press* , Cambridge MA, **1986**

[76] **Sutherland, I E, Sproul, R F, Schumacker, R A** , *'A characterization of ten hidden-surface algorithms'* , ACM Comput. Surveys, Vol. 6 , **March 1974**, pp. 1–55

[77] **Widrow, B, Hoff, M E** , *'Adaptive switching circuits'* , IRE WESCON Conv. Record, Part 4 **Aug. 1960** , pp. 96–104

[78] **Widrow, B, Winter, R G, Baxter, R** , *'Learning phenomena in layered neural networks'* , IEEE 1st Int. Conf. Neural Networks, San Diego CA, June 21–24, Vol. II , **1987** , pp. 411–429

[79] **Williams, H P** , *"Fourier's method of linear programming and its dual"* , Amer. Math. Monthly, Vol. 93 , **1986** , pp. 681–695

[80] **Yoh-Han Pao, Dejan J Sobajic** , *'Nonlinear process control with neural nets'*, Neurocomputing, Vol. 2 , **1990** , pp. 51–59

[81] **Young, T Y, Calvert, T W** , *'Classification, estimation and pattern recognition'* , American Elsevier Publishing Company, Inc., New York, London, Amsterdam.

Anhang A

Programmausdruck

```
C ***********************************************************************
C *                                                                     *
C ***********************************************************************

      PROGRAM TEST

C ***********************************************************************
C *   THIS IS THE MAIN PROGRAM.                                         *
C *   ITS PURPOSE IS JUST TO SET UP SOME GLOBAL PARAMETERS,             *
C *   CALL THE SUBROUTINE LUNS, WHICH ACTUALLY DOES ALL THE             *
C *   WORK, AND WRITE THE RESULTS IN A FILE FOR FURTHER USE.            *
C ***********************************************************************


C ***********************************************************************
C *   IN THE FOLLOWING THE GLOBAL PARAMETERS ARE DECLARED.             *
C *   FORTRAN DOES NOT ALLOW DYNAMIC ALLOCATION OF STORAGE.            *
C *   SINCE WE WOULD LIKE TO LET M AND N VARY FREELY,                  *
C *   WITHIN SOME BOUNDS, WE HAVE TO RESORT TO THE FOLLOWING  TRICK:   *
C *   FIND NNMAX, MMAX AND LET 1 < N < NMAX, 1 < M < MMAX.            *
C *   DECLARE THE MATRIX A IN THE MAIN PROGRAM AS AN ONE-DIM. ARRAY   *
C *   OF LENTH NMAX * MMAX BUT USE IT AS A TWO DIMENSIONAL MATRIX     *
C *   OF DIMENSIONS M, N IN THE SUBROUTINE.                            *
C *   NOW, TOTAL STORAGE REQUIRED IS APPROXX. EQUAL TO                 *
C *   3*N*N+4*M*M+5*M*N+26*N+28*M+12  ::MEM(M,N)                       *
C *   A TERRIFIC QUADRATIC FORM FROM WHICH, IF YOU HAVE TIME TO WASTE, *
C *   YOU MAY COMPUTE NMAX, MMAX.                                       *
C *   I SET MEM(M,N)= 3*N*N+4*M*M (I.E. I IGNORED THE LINEAR TERMS).   *
C *   YOU GET NMAX BY SETTING M=0 : NMAX=SQRT(MEM(M,N))/SQRT(3)        *
C *   AND SIMILARLY FOR MMAX:  MMAX=SQRT(MEM(M,N))/2                    *
C *   THE PARAMETER SQRMEM BELOW IS EXACTLY SQRT(MEM(M,N)).            *
C *   IT GETS A LARGE VALUE, SAY 700.                                   *
C *   THE REST IS THEN CLEAR (I THINK)                                  *
C ***********************************************************************

      PARAMETER(SQRMEM=700,SQRT3=1.73205)
      PARAMETER(NMAX=SQRMEM/SQRT3,MMAX=SQRMEM/2.)
      PARAMETER(MN=(SQRMEM*SQRMEM)/(8.*SQRT3))

C ***********************************************************************
C *   THE UNIFORM DISTRIBUTION IN [R1,R2] IS USED IN THE TESTS.        *
C *   ITMAX: MAXIMUM NUMBER OF ITERATIONS ALLOWED IN THE               *
C *   SIMPLEX METHOD (I.E. ROUTINE EO4MBF)                             *
C *   MSGLVL: SEE NAG MANUAL FOR EO4MBF                                *
C *   RHO : THE RHO-PARAMETER IN THE HO-KASHYAP METHOD                 *
C ***********************************************************************

      PARAMETER(R1=-1.,R2=1.,COSMAX=0.05,NTESMX=100)
      PARAMETER(ITMAX=100000,MSGLVL=0,RHO=0.9)

C ***********************************************************************
C *   THE MAIN PROBLEM IS: FIND A W SO THAT AW > O.                    *
C *   SOMETIMES WE WILL SOLVE AW + B > = O, SO WE NEED A B TOO.        *
C *   THE NORMS OF THE ROWS OF A WILL BE STORED IN ANORMS.             *
```

```
C *    APLUS IS THE GENERALIZED INVERSE OF A.                      *
C *    C IS JUST A COPY OF SOME ROW OF A.                          *
C *    R WILL HOLD THE RESIDUE AW-B.                               *
C *    ACOPY WILL HOLD A COPY OF A OR THE TRANSPOSE OF THE GENERALISED *
C *    INVERSE OF A (THAT'S WHAT FO1BLF COMPUTES)                  *
C *    AIJMX, D, U, DU, AIJMX1, D1, U1, DU1, INC,INC1 ARE USED BY FO6BLF*
C *    AS WORKING SPACE.                                           *
C *****************************************************************

       REAL*8 A(MN),W(NMAX),B(MMAX),ANORMS(MMAX),WSTAR(NMAX)
       REAL*8 APLUS(MN),C(NMAX),R(MMAX),ACOPY(MN)
       REAL*8 AIJMX(NMAX),D(MMAX),U(NMAX,NMAX),DU(NMAX)
       REAL*8 AIJMX1(MMAX),D1(NMAX),U1(MMAX,MMAX),DU1(MMAX)
       INTEGER INC(NMAX),INC1(MMAX)


C *****************************************************************
C *    I COMPUTED MN1 BY COUNTING THE ELEMENTS OF A1.              *
C *    A1 IS THE MATRIX OF THE LINEAR CONSTRAINTS IN SIMPLEX1.     *
C *    OF COURSE, MN1 IS DEPENDENT ON SQRMEM.                      *
C *    I HAD TO COMPUTE AN NMAX FOR THE SIMPLEX 1 -- CALL IT NMAX1. *
C *    NTOTM1, LIWM1: MAXIMUM VALUES FOR THE CORRESPONDING PARAMETERS *
C *    REQUIRED BY EO4MBF (ALSO LWOM1)                             *
C *    BL1, BU1 : HOLD LOWER AND UPPER BOUNDS OF THE VARIABLES AND *
C *    THE CONSTRAINTS.                                            *
C *    CVEC1 IS THE VEKTOR DEFINING THE OBJECTIVE FUNCTION         *
C *    OBJLP1 HOLDS THE VALUE OF THE OBJECTIVE FUNCTION UPON EXIT. *
C *    CLAMD1 HOLDS THE LAGRNGE-MULTIPLIERS UPON EXIT.             *
C *    WORK1, ISTAT1, IWORK1 : WORKING SPACE AND STATUS VARIABLES. *
C *****************************************************************

       PARAMETER(MN1=(SQRMEM+SQRT3)*(SQRMEM+SQRT3)/(8.*SQRT3))
       PARAMETER(NMAX1=NMAX+1,NTOTM1=NMAX+1,LIWM1=2*NMAX1)
       PARAMETER(LWOM1=2*NMAX*NMAX+10*NMAX+8)
       REAL*8 A1(MN1),X1(NMAX1),BL1(NTOTM1),BU1(NTOTM1)
       REAL*8 CVEC1(NMAX1),OBJLP1,CLAMD1(NTOTM1),WORK1(LWOM1)
       INTEGER ISTAT1(NTOTM1),IWORK1(LIWM1)


C *****************************************************************
C *    SIMPLEX 2 VARIABLES: THE SIMPLEX 1 COMMENTS APPLY FULLY HERE TOO.*
C *****************************************************************

       PARAMETER(MN2=MMAX*MMAX)
       PARAMETER(NMAX2=NMAX,NTOTM2=2*MMAX,LIWM2=2*NMAX2)
       PARAMETER(LWOM2=2*MMAX*MMAX+11*MMAX)
       REAL*8 A2(MN2),X2(NMAX2),BL2(NTOTM2),BU2(NTOTM2)
       REAL*8 CVEC2(NMAX2),OBJLP2,CLAMD2(NTOTM2),WORK2(LWOM2)
       INTEGER ISTAT2(NTOTM2),IWORK2(LIWM2)


C *****************************************************************
C *    VARIABLES FOR TIME STATISTICS:                             *
C *    TRAND : TIME REQUIRED FOR RANDOM NUMBER GENERATION.         *
C *    TPER  :    -- // --      PERCEPTRON RULE                    *
C *    TRELAX:    -- // --      RELAXATION RULE                    *
C *    THOKA :    -- // --      HO-KASHYAP RULE                    *
C *    TSIMP1:    -- // --      SIMPLEX 1                          *
```

```
C *    TSIMP2     -- // --     SIMPLEX 2                              *
C *    THE ABOVE WILL HOLD THE MEASURED TIMES FOR MAXIMALLY           *
C *    NTESMX TESTS. HERE (SEE ABOVE) NTESMX=100 BUT WE ARE ACTUALLY  *
C *    GOING TO DO ONLY NTESTS=10 TESTS EACH TIME (HERE YOU CLEARLY   *
C *    SEE THE DIFFERENCE BETWEEN MAXIMALLY ALLOWED AND ACTUALLY USED *
C *    --- THAT'S FORTRAN!)                                           *
C *    THE VARIABLES MRAND, MPER ETC. WILL HOLD THE MEAN TIMES        *
C *    WHILE THE S-VARIABLES (SRAND, SPER ETC) WILL HOLD THE          *
C *    STANDARD DEVIATIONS.                                           *
C *    WT IS AGAIN SOME WORKING SPACE.                                *
C ********************************************************************

       REAL*8 TRAND(NTESMX),TPER(NTESMX),TRELAX(NTESMX),THOKA(NTESMX)
       REAL*8 TSIMP1(NTESMX),TSIMP2(NTESMX)
       REAL*8 MRAND,MPER,MRELAX,MHOKA
       REAL*8 MSIMP1,MSIMP2
       REAL*8 SRAND,SPER,SRELAX,SHOKA
       REAL*8 SSIMP1,SSIMP2
       REAL*8 WT(NTESMX)
C ---
C --- VARIOUS CONSTANTS
       REAL*8 R1,R2,COSMAX,RHO




C ********************************************************************
C *    EXECUTABLE CODE STARTS HERE.                                  *
C *    WHAT WE DO IS JUST OPEN A FILE TO WRITE THE TIMES,            *
C *    START THE LOOPS IN N AND M (THE LIMIT FOR M DEPENDS ON N      *
C *    TROUGH AN OBSCURE FORMULA DICTATED BY SPACE REQUIREMENTS),    *
C *    CALL LUNS ([L]INEARE [UN]GLEICHUNGS[S]YSTEME) TO DO THE WORK, *
C *    PASS TO IT ALL PARAMETERS THAT WE WILL NEED AND, UPON EXIT,   *
C *    WRITE THE RESULTS IN THE FILE.                                *
C *    THE LIWRK- AND NCTOT- VARIABLES ARE NEEDE BY E04MBF.          *
C *    SEE THE NAG MANUAL FOR THEIR MEANING.                         *
C ********************************************************************

       OPEN(FILE='TIMES.LUNS',UNIT=18)
       DO 1 N=65,NMAX,5
       NTESTS=10
       N1=N+1
       LIWRK1=2*N1
       DO 2 M=5,MIN(125.,(SQRMEM-SQRT3*N)/2.),5
       IF(M.LT.40.AND.N.EQ.65)GOTO 2
       M1=M
       NCTOT1=M1+N1
       LWORK1=2*N1*N1+4*M1+6*N1+M1
       M2=M
       N2=M+N
       NCTOT2=M2+N2
       LIWRK2=2*N2
       LWORK2=2*(M2+1)*(M2+1)+4*M2+6*N2+M2

       CALL LUNS(M,N,R1,R2,NTESTS,ITMAX,MSGLVL,A,W,B,ANORMS,APLUS,C,R,
      *ACOPY,AIJMX,D,U,DU,AIJMX1,D1,U1,DU1,INC,INC1,M1,N1,NCTOT1,LIWRK1,
```

```
      *LWORK1,A1,X1,BL1,BU1,CVEC1,OBJLP1,CLAMD1,WORK1,ISTAT1,IWORK1,
      *M2,N2,NCTOT2,LIWRK2,LWORK2,A2,X2,BL2,BU2,CVEC2,OBJLP2,CLAMD2,
      *WORK2,ISTAT2,IWORK2,TRAND,TPER,TRELAX,THOKA,TSIMP1,TSIMP2,MRAND,
      *MPER,MRELAX,MHOKA,MSIMP1,MSIMP2,SRAND,SPER,SRELAX,SHOKA,SSIMP1,
      *SSIMP2,WT,COSMAX,RHO,WSTAR)

C ***************** TO BE USED FOR TIME TESTS: ************************
      WRITE(18,8989)M,N,MRAND,SRAND,MPER,SPER,MRELAX,SRELAX,MHOKA,SHOKA,
      *MSIMP1,SSIMP1,MSIMP2,SSIMP2
      WRITE(2,8989)M,N,MRAND,SRAND,MPER,SPER,MRELAX,SRELAX,MHOKA,SHOKA,
      *MSIMP1,SSIMP1,MSIMP2,SSIMP2
8989  FORMAT(2(I4),12(F9.4))

2     CONTINUE
1     CONTINUE

      END




      SUBROUTINE LUNS(M,N,R1,R2,NTESTS,ITMAX,MSGLVL,
      *A,W,B,ANORMS,APLUS,C,R,
      *ACOPY,AIJMX,D,U,DU,AIJMX1,D1,U1,DU1,INC,INC1,M1,N1,NCTOT1,LIWRK1,
      *LWORK1,A1,X1,BL1,BU1,CVEC1,OBJLP1,CLAMD1,WORK1,ISTAT1,IWORK1,
      *M2,N2,NCTOT2,LIWRK2,LWORK2,A2,X2,BL2,BU2,CVEC2,OBJLP2,CLAMD2,
      *WORK2,ISTAT2,IWORK2,TRAND,TPER,TRELAX,THOKA,TSIMP1,TSIMP2,MRAND,
      *MPER,MRELAX,MHOKA,MSIMP1,MSIMP2,SRAND,SPER,SRELAX,SHOKA,SSIMP1,
      *SSIMP2,WT,COSMAX,RHO,WSTAR)
C ---
C     TOTAL STORAGE REQUIRED IS APPROX. EQUAL TO
C     3*N*N+4*M*M+5*M*N+26*N+28*M+12
C ---

C **********************************************************************
C *   SEE THE COMMENTS IN THE MAIN PROGRAM FOR THE                     *
C *   DECLARATIONS PART.                                               *
C **********************************************************************

      REAL*8 A(M,N),W(N),B(M),ANORMS(M),APLUS(N,M),C(N),R(M),ACOPY(M,N)
      REAL*8 WSTAR(N)
      REAL*8 AIJMX(N),D(M),U(N,N),DU(N)
      REAL*8 AIJMX1(M),D1(N),U1(M,M),DU1(M)
      INTEGER INC(N),INC1(M)
C ---
      REAL*8 A1(M1,N1),X1(N1),BL1(NCTOT1),BU1(NCTOT1)
      REAL*8 CVEC1(N1),OBJLP1,CLAMD1(NCTOT1),WORK1(LWORK1)
      INTEGER ISTAT1(NCTOT1),IWORK1(LIWRK1)
C ---
      REAL*8 A2(M2,N2),X2(N2),BL2(NCTOT2),BU2(NCTOT2)
```

```
      REAL*8 CVEC2(N2),OBJLP2,CLAMD2(NCTOT2),WORK2(LWORK2)
      INTEGER ISTAT2(NCTOT2),IWORK2(LIWRK2)
C ---
C --- TIMES
      REAL*8 TRAND(NTESTS),TPER(NTESTS),TRELAX(NTESTS),THOKA(NTESTS)
      REAL*8 TSIMP1(NTESTS),TSIMP2(NTESTS)
      REAL*8 MRAND,MPER,MRELAX,MHOKA
      REAL*8 MSIMP1,MSIMP2
      REAL*8 SRAND,SPER,SRELAX,SHOKA
      REAL*8 SSIMP1,SSIMP2
      REAL*8 WT(NTESTS),S3,S4,WTSUM
C ---
C --- VARIOUS CONSTANTS
      REAL*8 CONST,ALPHA,COEFF,BETA,XMAX,XMIN,TOL,EPS,XXXX,R1,R2,COSMAX
      REAL*8 COSCW,RHO,TTOOSM,TTOOLG,BMIN,SCALPR
      REAL*8 FO6EAF,FO6EJF,XO2AAF,FO6QGF,FO6FAF
      CHARACTER*1 TRANS,MATRIX,NORM,TRANSA,TRANSB
      CHARACTER*72 STARS
      LOGICAL LINOBJ

      INTEGER*4 STD,MINUT,SEC,ZTDL
      CHARACTER*45 SCRATCH

C ***********************************************************************
C *   NAG ROUTINES --- SEE NAG MANUAL.                                  *
C ***********************************************************************

      EXTERNAL FO6EAF,FO6EJF,XO2AAF,FO6QGF,FO6FAF

C ***********************************************************************
C *   EXECUTABLE CODE STARTS HERE.                                      *
C *   LINOBJ=.TRUE. MEANS WE ARE TRUELY GOING TO SOLVE A LINEAR         *
C *   PROGRAMMING PROBLEM (EO4MBF NEEDS TO KNOW)                        *
C ***********************************************************************

      INCX=1
      LINOBJ=.TRUE.
      STARS=                                                          '
      ***********************************************************************
      *******'
C***********************************************************************

C ***********************************************************************
C *   START THE TESTS!                                                  *
C ***********************************************************************

      DO 408 ITEST=1,NTESTS




C ***********************************************************************
C *   GEPRTINT RETURNS THE ABSOLUTE TIME (IN HOURS, MINUTES, SECONDS    *
C *   AND TEN-THOUSANDTHS OF A SECOND).                                 *
```

```
C *********************************************************************
      CALL GEPRTINT(STD,MINUT,SEC,ZTDL,SCRATCH)
      TSTART=60.*MINUT+SEC+(ZTDL/10000.)

C*********************************************************************

C --- RANDOM VECTOR GENERATION

C --- GENERATES A REPEATABLE SEQUENCE
C       CALL GO5CBF(100)

C --- GENERATES A NON-REPEATABLE SEQUENCE
      CALL GO5CCF

C --- GENERATION OF A CONSISTENT SYSTEM:

C --- REMOVE COMMENT FROM GOTO SATEMENT TO SKIP THIS SECTION
C       GOTO 401


C *********************************************************************
C *   GO5FAF GENERATES A VECTOR OF PSEUDO-RANDOM NUMBERS UNIFORMLY   *
C *   DISTRIBUTED OVER THE INTERVALL [R1,R2].                        *
C *   FO6EAF RETURNS THE SCALAR PRODUCT OF TWO VECTORS              *
C *********************************************************************

      K=0
      TOL=0.
      BMIN=1.E+20

C *********************************************************************
C *   CHOOSE AN INITIAL VECTOR WSTAR.                                *
C *********************************************************************

      CALL GO5FAF(R1,R2,N,WSTAR)

C *********************************************************************
C *   FOR EACH ONE OF THE M ROWS THAT WE HAVE TO FIND...             *
C *********************************************************************

      DO 70 I=1,M

C *********************************************************************
C *   CHOOSE A FUTHER VECTOR C...                                    *
C *********************************************************************

71    CALL GO5FAF(R1,R2,N,C)

C *********************************************************************
C *   COMPUTE THE SCALAR PRODUCT <C,WSTAR> AND IF IT'S NEGATIVE OR O  *
C *   GO BACK AND CHOOSE ANOTHER C.                                  *
C *********************************************************************

      SCALPR=FO6EAF(N,C,INCX,WSTAR,INCX)
```

```
      IF(SCALPR.LE.O.)GOTO 71

C ***********************************************************************
C *   IF YOU WANT A DIFFICULT SOLVABLE SYSTEM TRY THE FOLLOWING:       *
C *   COMPUTE COS(C,WSTAR) AND CHOOSE ANOTHER C IF                     *
C *   <C,WSTAR> < = O OR COS(C,WSTAR) > COSMAX                         *
C *   FOR SMALL COSMAX YOU WILL GET THE C VECTORS ON THE POSITIVE SIDE *
C *   BUT VERY CLOSE TO THE LINEAR SUBSPACE ORTHOGONAL TO WSTAR.       *
C ***********************************************************************

C     COSCW=F06FAF(N,K,TOL,C,INCX,TOL,WSTAR,INCX)
C     IF(SCALPR.LE.O..OR.COSCW.GE.COSMAX)GOTO 71

C ***********************************************************************
C *   BMIN IS THE MINIMUM SCALAR PRODUCT.                              *
C ***********************************************************************

      IF(BMIN.GT.SCALPR)BMIN=SCALPR

C ***********************************************************************
C *   IF O.K. THE VECTOR C WILL BECOME THE M-TH ROW OF A.             *
C ***********************************************************************

      DO 72 J=1,N
      A(I,J)=C(J)
72    CONTINUE
70    CONTINUE

401   CONTINUE

C --- GENERATION OF AN INCONSISTENT SYSTEM:

C --- REMOVE COMMENT FROM GOTO SATEMENT TO SKIP THIS SECTION
      GOTO 402


C ***********************************************************************
C *   FO6FBF PERFORMS THE OPERATION DU <---- (CONST,...,CONST)         *
C *   SO WE HAVE DU=0 (DU IS A VECTOR).                                *
C ***********************************************************************

      CONST=0.
      CALL FO6FBF(N,CONST,DU,INCX)
      ALPHA=-1.

      CALL GO5FAF(R1,R2,N,WSTAR)

C ***********************************************************************
C *   THE FIRST M-1 ROWS OF A WILL BE ON THE POSITIVE SIDE OF WSTAR... *
C ***********************************************************************

      DO 270 I=1,M-1
271   CALL GO5FAF(R1,R2,N,C)
      SCALPR=F06EAF(N,C,INCX,WSTAR,INCX)
      IF(SCALPR.LE.O.)GOTO 271
```

```
      DO 272 J=1,N
      A(I,J)=C(J)
272   CONTINUE

C ***********************************************************************
C *   FO6ECF PERFORMS THE OPERATION DU <---- ALPHA*C + DU, SO          *
C *   AT THE END DU WILL BE EQUAL TO MINUS THE SUM OF ALL C'S          *
C *   (ALPHA=-1)                                                       *
C ***********************************************************************

      CALL FO6ECF(N,ALPHA,C,INCX,DU,INCX)
270   CONTINUE

C ***********************************************************************
C *   THE M-TH LINE OF A WILL BE DU.                                   *
C *   THIS GUARANTEES INSOLVABILITY!                                   *
C ***********************************************************************

      DO 273 J=1,N
      A(M,J)=DU(J)
273   CONTINUE

402   CONTINUE

C***********************************************************************


C ***********************************************************************
C *   ASK THE TIME                                                     *
C ***********************************************************************

      CALL GEPRTINT(STD,MINUT,SEC,ZTDL,SCRATCH)
      RT1=60.*MINUT+SEC+(ZTDL/10000.)
      TRAND(ITEST)=RT1-TSTART

C ***********************************************************************
C *   FOR A DETAILED OUTPUT:                                           *
C ***********************************************************************

C --- REMOVE COMMENT FROM GOTO SATEMENT TO SKIP THIS SECTION
      GOTO 403

      WRITE(2,*)STARS
      WRITE(2,*)'PROBLEM: FIND A SOLUTION VECTOR W TO THE INEQUALITIES:
     *A*W>0'
      WRITE(2,*)'THE MATRIX A IS:'
      DO 100 I=1,M
      WRITE(2,101)(A(I,J),J=1,N)
101   FORMAT(1X,40(F7.4,1X))
100   CONTINUE
      WRITE(2,*)'TIME NEEDED TO GENERATE RANDOMLY THE MATRIX A:',TRAND(I
     *TEST),' SEC'
      WRITE(2,*)STARS

403   CONTINUE
```

```
      CALL GEPRTINT(STD,MINUT,SEC,ZTDL,SCRATCH)
      TSTART=60.*MINUT+SEC+(ZTDL/10000.)

C --- SOLUTION METHODS:

C --- IN CASE OF AN INCONSISTENT SYSTEM REMOVE COMMENT FROM
C --- GOTO SATEMENT TO SKIP THE PERCEPTRON AND RELAXATION PROCEDURES
C       GOTO 405

C***********************************************************************
C --- PERCEPTRON PROCEDURE
      ALPHA=1.

C ***********************************************************************
C *   STARTVECTOR W IS 0.                                              *
C ***********************************************************************

      CONST=0.
      CALL F06FBF(N,CONST,W,INCX)
      ITER=0
5     IFAIL=0

C ***********************************************************************
C *   START NEW CYCLE.                                                 *
C ***********************************************************************

      ITER=ITER+1

C ***********************************************************************
C *   FOR EACH ROW OF A...                                            *
C ***********************************************************************

      DO 2 I=1,M

C ***********************************************************************
C *   COPY IT IN C...                                                 *
C ***********************************************************************

      DO 3 J=1,N
      C(J)=A(I,J)
3     CONTINUE

C ***********************************************************************
C *   AND IF <C,W> < = 0 ...                                          *
C ***********************************************************************

      IF(F06EAF(N,C,INCX,W,INCX).LE.0.)THEN
      IFAIL=1

C ***********************************************************************
C *   ADD C TO W (F06ECF PERFORMS THE TASK W <--- ALPHA*C + W)        *
C ***********************************************************************

      CALL F06ECF(N,ALPHA,C,INCX,W,INCX)
```

```
      ENDIF
2     CONTINUE

C *********************************************************************
C *  IF W FAILED    TO  BE  A  SOLUTION, START  A NEW CYCLE.        *
C *********************************************************************

      IF(IFAIL.EQ.1)GOTO 5
C*********************************************************************



C *********************************************************************
C *  ASK THE TIME.                                                    *
C *********************************************************************

      CALL GEPRTINT(STD,MINUT,SEC,ZTDL,SCRATCH)
      RT1=60.*MINUT+SEC+(ZTDL/10000.)
      TPER(ITEST)=RT1-TSTART


C *********************************************************************
C *  FOR DETAILED OUTPUT:                                             *
C *********************************************************************

C --- REMOVE COMMENT FROM GOTO SATEMENT TO SKIP THIS SECTION
      GOTO 404

      WRITE(2,*)STARS
      WRITE(2,*)'SOLUTION FOUND BY THE PERCEPTRON PROCEDURE:'
      WRITE(2,101)(W(I),I=1,N)

C --- VERIFICATION
      TRANS='N'
      ALPHA=1.
      BETA=0.
      CALL FO6PAF(TRANS,M,N,ALPHA,A,M,W,INCX,BETA,B,INCX)
      WRITE(2,*)'VERIFICATION: THE VECTOR A*W IS EQUAL TO'
      WRITE(2,101)(B(I),I=1,M)
C --- VERIFICATION END

      WRITE(2,*)'NUMBER OF CYCLES:',ITER
      WRITE(2,*)'TIME NEEDED TO FIND THE ABOVE SOLUTION:',TPER(ITEST),
     *' SEC'
      WRITE(2,*)STARS

404   CONTINUE

      CALL GEPRTINT(STD,MINUT,SEC,ZTDL,SCRATCH)
      TSTART=60.*MINUT+SEC+(ZTDL/10000.)

C*********************************************************************

C --- RELAXATION PROCEDURE
```

```
C ******************************************************************
C *   FOR EACH ROW OF A...                                        *
C ******************************************************************

      DO 7 I=1,M

C ******************************************************************
C *   COPY IT IN C...                                             *
C ******************************************************************

      DO 8 J=1,N
      C(J)=A(I,J)
8     CONTINUE

C ******************************************************************
C *   AND COMPUTE THE NORM OF IT (AND STORE ITS SQUARE IN ANORMS) *
C ******************************************************************

      ANORMS(I)=F06EJF(N,C,INCX)
      ANORMS(I)=ANORMS(I)*ANORMS(I)
7     CONTINUE

C ******************************************************************
C *   WE USE LAMDA=2 AND B=0, W=0 AS STARTING VECTORS FOR B AND W *
C ******************************************************************

      LAMDA=2
      CONST=1.
      CALL F06FBF(M,CONST,B,INCX)
      CONST=0.
      CALL F06FBF(N,CONST,W,INCX)
      ITER=0
15    IFAIL=0

C ******************************************************************
C *   START A NEW CYCLE.                                          *
C ******************************************************************

      ITER=ITER+1

C ******************************************************************
C *   FOR EACH ROW OF A...                                        *
C ******************************************************************

      DO 12 I=1,M

C ******************************************************************
C *   COPY IT IN C...                                             *
C ******************************************************************

      DO 13 J=1,N
      C(J)=A(I,J)
13    CONTINUE

C ******************************************************************
```

```
C *   AND COMPUTE THE DIFFERENCE <C,W>-B(I).                              *
C ****************************************************************************

      DIFF=FO6EAF(N,C,INCX,W,INCX)-B(I)

C ****************************************************************************
C *   IF IT IS LOWER THAN ZERO...                                          *
C ****************************************************************************

      IF(DIFF.LT.O.)THEN
      IFAIL=1
      COEFF=-LAMDA*DIFF/ANORMS(I)

C ****************************************************************************
C *   ADD COEFF*C TO W.                                                    *
C ****************************************************************************

      CALL FO6ECF(N,COEFF,C,INCX,W,INCX)
      ENDIF
12    CONTINUE

C ****************************************************************************
C *   IF W FAILED TO BE A SOLUTION, START A NEW CYCLE.                     *
C ****************************************************************************

      IF(IFAIL.EQ.1)GOTO 15
C****************************************************************************


C ****************************************************************************
C *   ASK THE TIME.                                                        *
C ****************************************************************************

      CALL GEPRTINT(STD,MINUT,SEC,ZTDL,SCRATCH)
      RT1=60.*MINUT+SEC+(ZTDL/10000.)
      TRELAX(ITEST)=RT1-TSTART


C ****************************************************************************
C *   FOR A DETAILED OUTPUT:                                               *
C ****************************************************************************

C --- REMOVE COMMENT FROM GOTO SATEMENT TO SKIP THIS SECTION
      GOTO 405

      WRITE(2,*)STARS
      WRITE(2,*)'SOLUTION FOUND BY THE RELAXATION PROCEDURE:'
      WRITE(2,101)(W(I),I=1,N)

C --- VERIFICATION
      TRANS='N'
      ALPHA=1.
      BETA=0.
      CALL FO6PAF(TRANS,M,N,ALPHA,A,M,W,INCX,BETA,B,INCX)
      WRITE(2,*)'VERIFICATION: THE VECTOR A*W IS EQUAL TO'
```

```
      WRITE(2,101)(B(I),I=1,M)
C --- VERIFICATION END

      WRITE(2,*)'NUMBER OF CYCLES:',ITER
      WRITE(2,*)'TIME NEEDED TO FIND THE ABOVE SOLUTION:',TRELAX(ITEST),
     *' SEC'
      WRITE(2,*)STARS

405   CONTINUE

      CALL GEPRTINT(STD,MINUT,SEC,ZTDL,SCRATCH)
      TSTART=60.*MINUT+SEC+(ZTDL/10000.)


C***********************************************************************

C --- HO-KASHYAP-PROCEDURE

C ***********************************************************************
C *   NEEDED BY NAG ROUTINES:                                          *
C ***********************************************************************

      MATRIX='G'
      NORM='F'

C ***********************************************************************
C *   EPS: THE SMALLEST POSITIVE NON-ZERO NUMBER REPRESENTABLE ON      *
C *   THE MACHINE.                                                     *
C ***********************************************************************

C ***********************************************************************

      EPS=X02AAF(XXXX)

C ***********************************************************************
C *   AN INITIAL GUESS FOR TOL:                                        *
C ***********************************************************************

C       TOL=EPS*F06QGF(NORM,MATRIX,M,N,A,M)
      TOL=N*1.E-06

C ***********************************************************************
C *   A TOO LARGE TOL:                                                 *
C ***********************************************************************

      TTOOLG=0.0001

C ***********************************************************************
C *   A TOO SMALL TOL:                                                 *
C ***********************************************************************

      TTOOSM=EPS


630   IFAIL=-1
```

```
C ********************************************************************
C *    IF N>M ...                                                    *
C ********************************************************************

      IF(N.GT.M)THEN

C ********************************************************************
C *    PUT THE TRANSPOSE OF A IN APLUS...                            *
C ********************************************************************

      DO 30 I=1,N
      DO 31 J=1,M
      APLUS(I,J)=A(J,I)
31    CONTINUE
30    CONTINUE

C ********************************************************************
C * CALL F01BLF TO COMPUTE THE TRANSPOSE OF THE PSEUDOINVERSE OF APLUS *
C ********************************************************************

      CALL F01BLF(N,M,TOL,APLUS,N,AIJMX1,IRANK,INC1,D1,U1,M,DU1,IFAIL)

C ********************************************************************
C *    THE PSEUDOINVERSE IS WRITTEN ON APLUS ITSELF, SO APLUS        *
C *    HOLDS NOW THE TRANSPOSE OF THE PSEUDOINVERSE OF THE TRANSPOSE *
C *    OF A, THAT IS: THE PSEUDOINVERSE OF A.    ALLES KLAR?         *
C ********************************************************************


C ********************************************************************
C *    BUT IF F01BLF FAILED TO COMPUTE THE PSEUDONVERSE BECAUSE OF TOL..*
C ********************************************************************

      IF(IFAIL.EQ.2)THEN
      WRITE(2,*)'HO-KASHYAP PROCEDURE: IFAIL=2 IN PSEUDOINVERSE COMPUTAT
     *ION'

C ********************************************************************
C *    IF IRANK=0 THE USED TOLERANCE TOL WAS TOO LARGE :             *
C ********************************************************************

      IF(IRANK.EQ.0)TTOOLG=TOL

C ********************************************************************
C *    IF IRANK >0 THE USED TOLERANCE TOL WAS TOO SMALL:             *
C ********************************************************************

      IF(IRANK.GT.0)TTOOSM=TOL

C ********************************************************************
C *    LET TOL BE IN THE MIDDLE OF CURRENT TOO LARGE AND TOO SMALL TOL'S*
C ********************************************************************

      TOL=(TTOOLG+TTOOSM)/2.
```

```
C ********************************************************************
C *    ... AND GO BACK TO TRY AGAIN.                                 *
C ********************************************************************

      GOTO 630
      ENDIF

C ********************************************************************
C *    ELSE (THAT IS, IF M > = N)...                                 *
C ********************************************************************

      ELSE

C ********************************************************************
C *    COPY A IN ACOPY...                                            *
C ********************************************************************

      CALL FO6QFF(MATRIX,M,N,A,M,ACOPY,M)

C ********************************************************************
C *    AND CALL FO1BLF TO COMPUTE THE TRANSPOSE OF THE PSEUDOINVERSE *
C *    OF ACOPY.                                                     *
C ********************************************************************

      CALL FO1BLF(M,N,TOL,ACOPY,M,AIJMX,IRANK,INC,D,U,N,DU,IFAIL)

C ********************************************************************
C *    ACOPY WILL BE OVERWRITTEN, SO ACOPY NOW HOLDS THE TRANSPOSE   *
C *    OF THE PSEUDOINVERSE OF A.   KLAR?                            *
C ********************************************************************


C ********************************************************************
C *    BUT IF FO1BLF FAILS TO DO ITS JOB BECAUSE OF INVALID TOL...   *
C ********************************************************************

      IF(IFAIL.EQ.2)THEN

C ********************************************************************
C *    START A BISECTION PROCEDURE ON TOL (SEE COMMENTS ABOVE)       *
C ********************************************************************

      IF(IRANK.EQ.0)TTOOLG=TOL
      IF(IRANK.GT.0)TTOOSM=TOL
      TOL=(TTOOLG+TTOOSM)/2.
      GOTO 630
      ENDIF

C ********************************************************************
C *    IF EVERYTHING WAS O.K., WRITE THE TRANSPOSE OF ACOPY IN APLUS. *
C ********************************************************************

      DO 32 I=1,N
      DO 33 J=1,M
      APLUS(I,J)=ACOPY(J,I)
```

```
33      CONTINUE
32      CONTINUE
        ENDIF

C *******************************************************************
C *    AT LAST, APLUS IS WHAT IT SHOULD BE : THE PSEUDOINVERSE OF A.  *
C *******************************************************************

        TRANS='N'

C *******************************************************************
C *    SET THE VECTOR B TO A VECTOR OF ONE'S : B <--- (CONST,...CONST)  *
C *******************************************************************

        CONST=1.
        CALL F06FBF(M,CONST,B,INCX)

C *******************************************************************
C *    PERFORM W <--- ALPHA*APLUS*B + BETA*W                         *
C *******************************************************************

        ALPHA=1.
        BETA=0.
        CALL F06PAF(TRANS,N,M,ALPHA,APLUS,N,B,INCX,BETA,W,INCX)

C *******************************************************************
C *    ... SO NOW THE INITIAL VECTOR W IS APLUS*B                    *
C *******************************************************************

        ITER=0
25      IFAIL=0

C *******************************************************************
C *    START A NEW CYCLE.                                            *
C *******************************************************************

        ITER=ITER+1

C *******************************************************************
C *    PERFORM R <--- ALPHA*A*W + BETA*R                             *
C *******************************************************************

        BETA=0.
        CALL F06PAF(TRANS,M,N,ALPHA,A,M,W,INCX,BETA,R,INCX)

C *******************************************************************
C *    ... SO R IS NOW A*W                                           *
C *******************************************************************


C *******************************************************************
C *    CHECK ALL THE COORDINATES OF R.                               *
C *******************************************************************

        DO 22 I=1,M
```

```
C *******************************************************************
C *   IF ONE IS NOT POSITIVE...                                     *
C *******************************************************************

      IF(R(I).LE.0.)THEN

C *******************************************************************
C *   PERFORM R <--- COEFF*B +R                                     *
C *******************************************************************

      COEFF=-1.
      CALL F06ECF(M,COEFF,B,INCX,R,INCX)

C *******************************************************************
C *   ...SO R IS NOW EQUAL TO A*W-B  R <--- R + |R|                 *
C *   THE FOLLOWING LOOP PERFORMS THE OPERATION R <--- R + |R|      *
C *******************************************************************

      DO 23 J=1,M
      IF(R(J).LE.0.)THEN
      R(J)=0.
      IFAIL=IFAIL+1
      ELSE
      R(J)=2.*R(J)
      ENDIF
23    CONTINUE

C *******************************************************************
C *   ...SO WE HAVE  NOW R = A*W-B + |A*W-B|                        *
C *   IF ALL COMPONENTS OF R ARE ZERO THE SYSTEM IS NOT SOLVABLE.   *
C *******************************************************************

      IF(IFAIL.EQ.M)THEN
      WRITE(2,*)'THE SYSTEM IS INCONSISTENT'
      GOTO 170
      ENDIF

C *******************************************************************
C *   ...OTERWISE PERFORM W <--- RHO*APLUS*R + BETA*W               *
C *******************************************************************

      BETA=1.
      CALL F06PAF(TRANS,N,M,RHO,APLUS,N,R,INCX,BETA,W,INCX)

C *******************************************************************
C *   ...AND B <--- RHO*R + B                                       *
C *******************************************************************

      CALL F06ECF(M,RHO,R,INCX,B,INCX)

C *******************************************************************
C *   ...AND START ANOTHER CYCLE.                                   *
C *******************************************************************
```

```
        GOTO 25
        ENDIF
22      CONTINUE
C*********************************************************************


C *******************************************************************
C *   ASK THE TIME.                                                 *
C *******************************************************************

170     CALL GEPRTINT(STD,MINUT,SEC,ZTDL,SCRATCH)
        RT1=60.*MINUT+SEC+(ZTDL/10000.)
        THOKA(ITEST)=RT1-TSTART


C *******************************************************************
C *   FOR DETAILED OUTPUT:                                          *
C *******************************************************************

C --- REMOVE COMMENT FROM GOTO SATEMENT TO SKIP THIS SECTION
        GOTO 406

        WRITE(2,*)STARS
        WRITE(2,*)'SOLUTION FOUND BY THE HO-KASHYAP PROCEDURE:'
        WRITE(2,101)(W(I),I=1,N)

C --- VERIFICATION
        TRANS='N'
        ALPHA=1.
        BETA=0.
        CALL F06PAF(TRANS,M,N,ALPHA,A,M,W,INCX,BETA,B,INCX)
        WRITE(2,*)'VERIFICATION: THE VECTOR A*W IS EQUAL TO'
        WRITE(2,101)(B(I),I=1,M)
        WRITE(2,*)'THE GENERALIZED INVERSE APLUS OF A IS:'
        DO 200 I=1,N
        WRITE(2,101)(APLUS(I,J),J=1,M)
200     CONTINUE
        WRITE(2,*)' '
        CALL F06YAF(TRANS,TRANS,M,M,N,ALPHA,A,M,APLUS,N,BETA,U1,M)
        CALL F06YAF(TRANS,TRANS,M,N,M,ALPHA,U1,M,A,M,BETA,ACOPY,M)
        WRITE(2,*)'VERIFICATION: THE MATRIX A*APLUS*A IS EQUAL TO'
        DO 201 I=1,M
        WRITE(2,101)(ACOPY(I,J),J=1,N)
201     CONTINUE
        WRITE(2,*)'...WHICH MUST BE EQUAL TO A'
        WRITE(2,*)' '
        CALL F06YAF(TRANS,TRANS,N,N,M,ALPHA,APLUS,N,A,M,BETA,U,N)
        WRITE(2,*)' '
        WRITE(2,*)'VERIFICATION: THE MATRIX APLUS*A IS EQUAL TO'
        DO 203 I=1,N
        WRITE(2,101)(U(I,J),J=1,N)
203     CONTINUE
        WRITE(2,*)'...WHICH MUST BE SYMMETRIC'
        WRITE(2,*)' '
        TRANSA='T'
```

```
      TRANSB='T'
      CALL F06YAF(TRANSA,TRANSB,M,N,N,ALPHA,APLUS,N,U,N,BETA,ACOPY,M)
      WRITE(2,*)'VERIFICATION: THE MATRIX APLUS*A*APLUS IS EQUAL TO'
      DO 202 J=1,N
      WRITE(2,101)(ACOPY(I,J),I=1,M)
202   CONTINUE
      WRITE(2,*)'...WHICH MUST BE EQUAL TO APLUS'
      WRITE(2,*)' '
C --- VERIFICATION END

      WRITE(2,*)'NUMBER OF CYCLES:',ITER
      WRITE(2,*)'TIME NEEDED TO FIND THE ABOVE SOLUTION:',THOKA(ITEST),
     *' SEC'
      WRITE(2,*)STARS

406   CONTINUE

      CALL GEPRTINT(STD,MINUT,SEC,ZTDL,SCRATCH)
      TSTART=60.*MINUT+SEC+(ZTDL/10000.)

C*********************************************************************

C --- SIMPLEX PROCEDURE (1ST METHOD)

C *******************************************************************
C *   SET B=(CONST,...,CONST) WITH CONST=1.                        *
C *******************************************************************

      CONST=1.
      CALL F06FBF(M,CONST,B,INCX)

C *******************************************************************
C *   SET UP THE MATRIX OF THE LINEAR CONSTRAINTS:                 *
C *******************************************************************

      DO 45 I=1,M1

C *******************************************************************
C *   THE FIRST N COLUMNS OF A1 ARE THE COLUMNS OF A.              *
C *******************************************************************

      DO 46 J=1,N
      A1(I,J)=A(I,J)
46    CONTINUE

C *******************************************************************
C *   THE LAST ONE IS A COLUMN OF ONE'S.                           *
C *******************************************************************

      A1(I,N1)=1.
45    CONTINUE

C *******************************************************************
C *   SET UP THE LOWER BOUNDS: THE FIRST N ARE -INFINITY,          *
C *   THE (N+1)-TH, WHICH IS THE N1-TH, IS 0 AND THE REST M ONES   *
```

```
C *    ARE EQUAL TO THE CORRESPONDING B-COORDINATE.                      *
C *********************************************************************

       DO 40 I=1,N
       BL1(I)=-1.0E+20
40     CONTINUE
       BL1(N1)=0.
       DO 41 I=N1+1,NCTOT1
       BL1(I)=B(I-N1)
41     CONTINUE

C *********************************************************************
C *    SET ALL UPPER BOUNDS TO +INFINITY:                             *
C *********************************************************************

       DO 42 I=1,NCTOT1
       BU1(I)=1.0E+20
42     CONTINUE

C *********************************************************************
C *    THE VECTOR CVEC1=(0,0,...0,1) DEFINES THE OBJECTIVE FUNCTION:  *
C *********************************************************************

       DO 43 I=1,N
       CVEC1(I)=0.
43     CONTINUE
       CVEC1(N1)=1.

C *********************************************************************
C *    THE VECTOR X1=(0,0,....,0,MAX(B(I))) IS AN INITIAL QUESS FOR X: *
C *********************************************************************

       DO 44 I=1,N
       X1(I)=0.
44     CONTINUE
       CALL F06FLF(M,B,INCX,XMAX,XMIN)
       X1(N1)=XMAX

C *********************************************************************
C *    CALL E04MBF TO FIND OPTIMAL X:                                 *
C *********************************************************************

       IFAIL=-1
       CALL E04MBF(ITMAX,MSGLVL,N1,M1,NCTOT1,M1,A1,BL1,BU1,CVEC1,LINOBJ,
      *X1,ISTAT1,OBJLP1,CLAMD1,IWORK1,LIWRK1,WORK1,LWORK1,IFAIL)
       IF(.NOT.(ABS(X1(N1)).LT.1000.*EPS))THEN
       WRITE(2,*)
       WRITE(2,*)'FIRST SIMPLEX METHOD : THE SYSTEM IS INCONSISTENT'
       WRITE(2,*)'X1(',N1,')=',X1(N1),'  IS BIGGER THAN ZERO'
       WRITE(2,*)STARS
       ENDIF
C*********************************************************************


C *********************************************************************
```

```
C *   ASK THE TIME                                                        *
C ***********************************************************************

      CALL GEPRTINT(STD,MINUT,SEC,ZTDL,SCRATCH)
      RT1=60.*MINUT+SEC+(ZTDL/10000.)
      TSIMP1(ITEST)=RT1-TSTART


C ***********************************************************************
C *   FOR DETAILED OUTPUT:                                              *
C ***********************************************************************

C --- REMOVE COMMENT FROM GOTO SATEMENT TO SKIP THIS SECTION
      GOTO 407

      WRITE(2,*)'SOLUTION FOUND BY THE 1ST SIMPLEX PROCEDURE:'
      WRITE(2,101)(X1(I),I=1,N)

C --- VERIFICATION
      TRANS='N'
      ALPHA=1.
      BETA=0.
      CALL F06PAF(TRANS,M1,N1,ALPHA,A1,M1,X1,INCX,BETA,B,INCX)
      WRITE(2,*)'VERIFICATION: THE VECTOR A1*X1 IS EQUAL TO'
      WRITE(2,101)(B(I),I=1,M1)
      WRITE(2,*)'A1 IS THE MATRIX OF THE LP'
      WRITE(2,*)'X1 IS THE SOLUTION VECTOR OF THE LP'
      WRITE(2,*)'NOTICE THAT A1*X1 IS BIGGER OR EQUAL TO THE B VECTOR'
      WRITE(2,*)'IN THIS CASE: EACH COMPONENT IS BIGGER OR EQUAL TO 1'
C --- VERIFICATION END

      WRITE(2,*)'TIME NEEDED TO FIND THE ABOVE SOLUTION:',TSIMP1(ITEST),
     *' SEC'
      WRITE(2,*)STARS

407   CONTINUE

      CALL GEPRTINT(STD,MINUT,SEC,ZTDL,SCRATCH)
      TSTART=60.*MINUT+SEC+(ZTDL/10000.)

C***********************************************************************

C --- SIMPLEX PROCEDURE (2ND METHOD)

C ***********************************************************************
C *   SET B=(CONST,...,CONST) WITH CONST=1:                             *
C ***********************************************************************

      CONST=1.
      CALL F06FBF(M,CONST,B,INCX)

C ***********************************************************************
C *   SET UP THE MATRIX OF THE LINEAR CONSTRAINTS A2:                   *
C ***********************************************************************
```

```
      DO 55 I=1,M2

C *********************************************************************
C *    THE FIRST N COLUMNS OF A2 ARE THE COLUMNS OF A:                *
C *********************************************************************

      DO 56 J=1,N
      A2(I,J)=A(I,J)
56    CONTINUE

C *********************************************************************
C *    THE REST M COLUMNS OF A2 FORM AN (M TIMES M) IDENTITY MATRIX:  *
C *********************************************************************

      DO 57 J=N+1,I+N-1
      A2(I,J)=0.
57    CONTINUE
      A2(I,I+N)=1.
      DO 58 J=I+N+1,N2
      A2(I,J)=0.
58    CONTINUE
55    CONTINUE

C *********************************************************************
C *    SET UP THE LOWER BOUNDS: THE FIRST N ARE -INFINITY...          *
C *********************************************************************

      DO 50 I=1,N
      BL2(I)=-1.0E+20
50    CONTINUE

C *********************************************************************
C *    ... THE NEXT M ARE ZERO...                                     *
C *********************************************************************

      DO 59 I=N+1,N2
      BL2(I)=0.
59    CONTINUE

C *********************************************************************
C *    ...AND THE NEXT M ARE EQUAL TO THE CORRESPONDING B-COORDINATES: *
C *********************************************************************

      DO 51 I=N2+1,NCTOT2
      BL2(I)=B(I-N2)
51    CONTINUE

C *********************************************************************
C *    SET ALL UPPER BOUNDS TO +INFINITY:                            *
C *********************************************************************

      DO 52 I=1,NCTOT2
      BU2(I)=1.0E+20
52    CONTINUE
```

```
C *********************************************************************
C *   THE VECTOR CVEC2=(0,0,...0,1,1,...1) DEFINES THE OBJECTIVE FUNCT.*
C *********************************************************************

      DO 53 I=1,N
      CVEC2(I)=0.
53    CONTINUE
      DO 60 I=N+1,N2
      CVEC2(I)=1.
60    CONTINUE


C *********************************************************************
C *   THE VECTOR X2=(0,0,...,0,B(1),...,B(M)) IS AN INITIAL GUESS:   *
C *********************************************************************

      DO 54 I=1,N
      X2(I)=0.
54    CONTINUE
      DO 61 I=N+1,N2
      X2(I)=B(I-N)
61    CONTINUE


C *********************************************************************
C *   CALL E04MBF TO FIND OPTIMAL X:                                 *
C *********************************************************************

      IFAIL=-1
      CALL E04MBF(ITMAX,MSGLVL,N2,M2,NCTOT2,M2,A2,BL2,BU2,CVEC2,LINOBJ,
     *X2,ISTAT2,OBJLP2,CLAMD2,IWORK2,LIWRK2,WORK2,LWORK2,IFAIL)
      DO 62 I=N+1,N2
      IF(.NOT.(ABS(X2(I)).LT.1000.*EPS))THEN
      WRITE(2,*)
      WRITE(2,*)'SECOND SIMPLEX METHOD : THE SYSTEM IS INCONSISTENT'
      WRITE(2,*)'X2(',I,')=',X2(I),'  IS BIGGER THAN ZERO'
      WRITE(2,*)STARS
      GOTO 63
      ENDIF
62    CONTINUE



C*********************************************************************


C *********************************************************************
C *   ASK THE TIME.                                                  *
C *********************************************************************

63    CALL GEPRTINT(STD,MINUT,SEC,ZTDL,SCRATCH)
      RT1=60.*MINUT+SEC+(ZTDL/10000.)
      TSIMP2(ITEST)=RT1-TSTART


C *********************************************************************
C *   FOR DETAILED OUTPUT:                                           *
C *********************************************************************
```

```
C --- REMOVE COMMENT FROM GOTO SATEMENT TO SKIP THIS SECTION
      GOTO 408

      WRITE(2,*)'SOLUTION FOUND BY THE 2ND SIMPLEX PROCEDURE:'
      WRITE(2,101)(X2(I),I=1,N)

C --- VERIFICATION
      TRANS='N'
      ALPHA=1.
      BETA=0.
      CALL FO6PAF(TRANS,M2,N2,ALPHA,A2,M2,X2,INCX,BETA,B,INCX)
      WRITE(2,*)'VERIFICATION: THE VECTOR A2*X2 IS EQUAL TO'
      WRITE(2,101)(B(I),I=1,M2)
      WRITE(2,*)'A2 IS THE MATRIX OF THE LP'
      WRITE(2,*)'X2 IS THE SOLUTION VECTOR OF THE LP'
      WRITE(2,*)'NOTICE THAT A2*X2 IS BIGGER OR EQUAL TO THE B VECTOR'
      WRITE(2,*)'IN THIS CASE: EACH COMPONENT IS BIGGER OR EQUAL TO 1'
C --- VERIFICATION END

      WRITE(2,*)'TIME NEEDED TO FIND THE ABOVE SOLUTION:',TSIMP2(ITEST),
     *' SEC'
      WRITE(2,*)STARS

408   CONTINUE

C*********************************************************************
C --- TIME STATISTICS

C *********************************************************************
C *   GO1AAF COMPUTES MEANS AND STANDARD DEVIATIONS:                 *
C *********************************************************************

      IFAIL=0
      IWT=0
      CALL GO1AAF(NTESTS,TRAND,IWT,WT,MRAND,SRAND,S3,S4,XMIN,XMAX,WTSUM,
     *IFAIL)
      CALL GO1AAF(NTESTS,TPER ,IWT,WT,MPER ,SPER ,S3,S4,XMIN,XMAX,WTSUM,
     *IFAIL)
      CALL GO1AAF(NTESTS,TRELAX,IWT,WT,MRELAX,SRELAX,S3,S4,XMIN,XMAX,
     *WTSUM,IFAIL)
      CALL GO1AAF(NTESTS,THOKA,IWT,WT,MHOKA,SHOKA,S3,S4,XMIN,XMAX,
     *WTSUM,IFAIL)
      CALL GO1AAF(NTESTS,TSIMP1,IWT,WT,MSIMP1,SSIMP1,S3,S4,XMIN,XMAX,
     *WTSUM,IFAIL)
      CALL GO1AAF(NTESTS,TSIMP2,IWT,WT,MSIMP2,SSIMP2,S3,S4,XMIN,XMAX,
     *WTSUM,IFAIL)
C*********************************************************************

      RETURN
      END
```

Anhang B

Probelauf

```
***********************************************************************
PROBLEM: FIND A SOLUTION VECTOR W TO THE INEQUALITIES: A*W>O
THE MATRIX A IS:
-0.0945 -0.3752 -0.1016 -0.8356  0.7418 -0.4841
 0.7938  0.7799 -0.5747  0.0477  0.7553  0.6333
 0.4854  0.1809  0.5994  0.6389  0.3550  0.4168
TIME NEEDED TO GENERATE RANDOMLY THE MATRIX A:0.13000369E-02 SEC
***********************************************************************
***********************************************************************
SOLUTION FOUND BY THE PERCEPTRON PROCEDURE:
 0.6992  0.4047 -0.6763 -0.7879  1.4971  0.1492
VERIFICATION: THE VECTOR A*W IS EQUAL TO
 1.5474  2.4470  0.0974
NUMBER OF CYCLES:2
TIME NEEDED TO FIND THE ABOVE SOLUTION:0.50002337E-03 SEC
***********************************************************************
***********************************************************************
SOLUTION FOUND BY THE RELAXATION PROCEDURE:
 1.3851  0.4518  0.3671 -0.0760  2.3339  0.5670
VERIFICATION: THE VECTOR A*W IS EQUAL TO
 1.1825  3.3590  1.9904
NUMBER OF CYCLES:3
TIME NEEDED TO FIND THE ABOVE SOLUTION:0.59998035E-03 SEC
***********************************************************************
***********************************************************************
SOLUTION FOUND BY THE HO-KASHYAP PROCEDURE:
 0.5554 -0.1337  0.5927 -0.1235  1.3126  0.0293
VERIFICATION: THE VECTOR A*W IS EQUAL TO
 1.0000  1.0000  1.0000
THE GENERALIZED INVERSE APLUS OF A IS:
 0.0581  0.2387  0.2585
-0.2872  0.3550 -0.2015
 0.2330 -0.4562  0.8159
-0.3762 -0.0981  0.3508
 0.6513  0.1808  0.4805
-0.2562  0.2204  0.0651


VERIFICATION: THE MATRIX A*APLUS*A IS EQUAL TO
-0.0945 -0.3752 -0.1016 -0.8356  0.7418 -0.4841
 0.7938  0.7799 -0.5747  0.0477  0.7553  0.6333
 0.4854  0.1809  0.5994  0.6389  0.3550  0.4168
```

...WHICH MUST BE EQUAL TO A

VERIFICATION: THE MATRIX APLUS*A IS EQUAL TO
 0.3095 0.2111 0.0119 0.1280 0.3152 0.2308
 0.2111 0.3481 -0.2956 0.1281 -0.0164 0.2798
 0.0119 -0.2956 0.7276 0.3049 0.1179 -0.0616
 0.1280 0.1281 0.3049 0.5338 -0.2286 0.2662
 0.3152 -0.0164 0.1179 -0.2286 0.7902 -0.0005
 0.2308 0.2798 -0.0616 0.2662 -0.0005 0.2908
...WHICH MUST BE SYMMETRIC

VERIFICATION: THE MATRIX APLUS*A*APLUS IS EQUAL TO
 0.0581 0.2387 0.2585
-0.2872 0.3550 -0.2015
 0.2330 -0.4562 0.8159
-0.3762 -0.0981 0.3508
 0.6513 0.1808 0.4805
-0.2562 0.2204 0.0651
...WHICH MUST BE EQUAL TO APLUS

NUMBER OF CYCLES:1
TIME NEEDED TO FIND THE ABOVE SOLUTION:0.69999695E-03 SEC
****

WORKSPACE PROVIDED IS   IW(14), W(155).
TO SOLVE PROBLEM WE NEED   IW(14), W(89).

EXIT LP PHASE.   INFORM = 0   ITER =   1

VARBL	STATE	VALUE	LOWER BOUND	UPPER BOUND	LAGR MULT	RESIDUAL
V 1	TB	0.0000000	NONE	NONE	-0.1481D-17	0.1000D+21
V 2	TB	0.0000000	NONE	NONE	-0.5878D-17	0.1000D+21
V 3	TB	0.0000000	NONE	NONE	-0.1593D-17	0.1000D+21
V 4	TB	0.0000000	NONE	NONE	-0.1309D-16	0.1000D+21
V 5	FR	1.872853	NONE	NONE	0.0000	0.1000D+21
V 6	FR	0.8040304	NONE	NONE	0.0000	0.1000D+21
V 7	LL	0.0000000	0.0000000	NONE	1.000	0.0000

LNCON	STATE	VALUE	LOWER BOUND	UPPER BOUND	LAGR MULT	RESIDUAL
L 1	LL	1.000000	1.000000	NONE	-0.1567D-16	-0.2637D-15
L 2	FR	1.923708	1.000000	NONE	0.0000	0.9237
L 3	LL	1.000000	1.000000	NONE	0.0000	-0.9714D-16

EXIT E04MBF - OPTIMAL LP SOLUTION FOUND.

LP OBJECTIVE FUNCTION =   4.163336D-17

NO. OF ITERATIONS =   1
SOLUTION FOUND BY THE 1ST SIMPLEX PROCEDURE:
 0.0000 0.0000 0.0000 0.0000 1.8729 0.8040

```
VERIFICATION: THE VECTOR A*W IS EQUAL TO
 1.0000  1.9237  1.0000
NOTICE THAT A*W IS BIGGER THAN THE B VECTOR
IN THIS CASE: EACH COMPONENT IS BIGGER OR EQUAL TO 1
TIME NEEDED TO FIND THE ABOVE SOLUTION:0.13599992E-01 SEC
**************************************************************************

WORKSPACE PROVIDED IS     IW(   18),  W(   101).
TO SOLVE PROBLEM WE NEED   IW(   18),  W(   101).

EXIT LP PHASE.   INFORM =  0   ITER =   3


VARBL STATE    VALUE     LOWER BOUND   UPPER BOUND   LAGR MULT   RESIDUAL

V  1   TB  0.0000000      NONE          NONE       -0.1497D-16  0.1000D+21
V  2   TB  0.0000000      NONE          NONE       -0.7749D-16  0.1000D+21
V  3   TB  0.0000000      NONE          NONE  '     0.1006D-15  0.1000D+21
V  4   FR  1.020090       NONE          NONE        0.0000      0.1000D+21
V  5   FR  1.955577       NONE          NONE        0.0000      0.1000D+21
V  6   FR -0.8300776      NONE          NONE        0.0000      0.1000D+21
V  7   LL  0.0000000    0.0000000       NONE        1.000       0.0000
V  8   LL  0.0000000    0.0000000       NONE        1.000       0.0000
V  9   LL  0.0000000    0.0000000       NONE        1.000       0.0000


LNCON STATE    VALUE     LOWER BOUND   UPPER BOUND   LAGR MULT   RESIDUAL

L  1   LL  1.000000     1.000000        NONE       -0.1039D-15  0.0000
L  2   LL  1.000000     1.000000        NONE        0.7559D-16 -0.5829D-15
L  3   LL  1.000000     1.000000        NONE       -0.1130D-15 -0.1804D-15

EXIT E04MBF - OPTIMAL LP SOLUTION FOUND.

LP OBJECTIVE FUNCTION =   4.163336D-17

NO. OF ITERATIONS =    3
SOLUTION FOUND BY THE 2ND SIMPLEX PROCEDURE:
 0.0000  0.0000  0.0000  1.0201  1.9556 -0.8301
VERIFICATION: THE VECTOR A*W IS EQUAL TO
 1.0000  1.0000  1.0000
NOTICE THAT A*W IS BIGGER THAN THE B VECTOR
IN THIS CASE: EACH COMPONENT IS BIGGER OR EQUAL TO 1
TIME NEEDED TO FIND THE ABOVE SOLUTION:0.14400005E-01 SEC
**************************************************************************
```

Appendix C

Zeit-Kurven

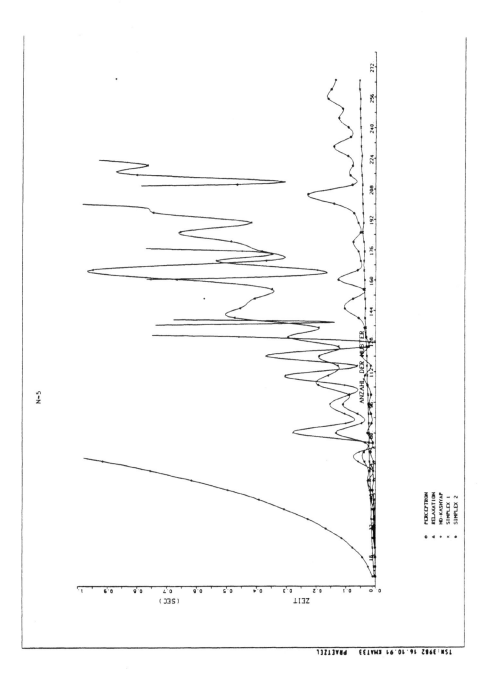

N-5

PERCEPTRON
RELAXATION
HO-KASHYAP
SIMPLEX 1
SIMPLEX 2

ANZAHL DER MUSTER

ZEIT (SEC)

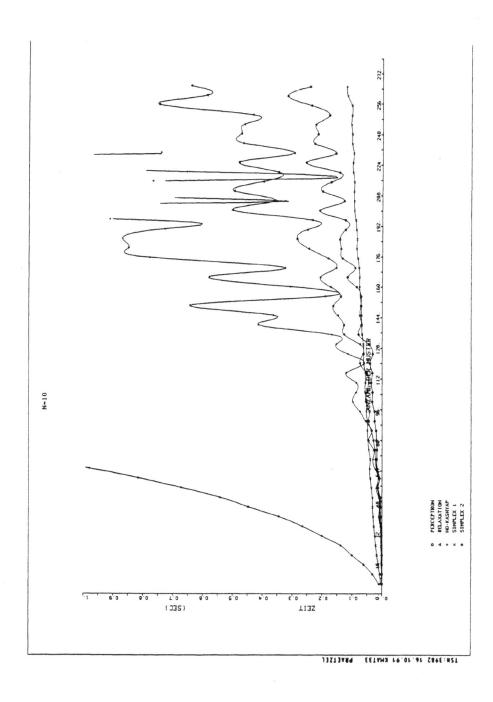

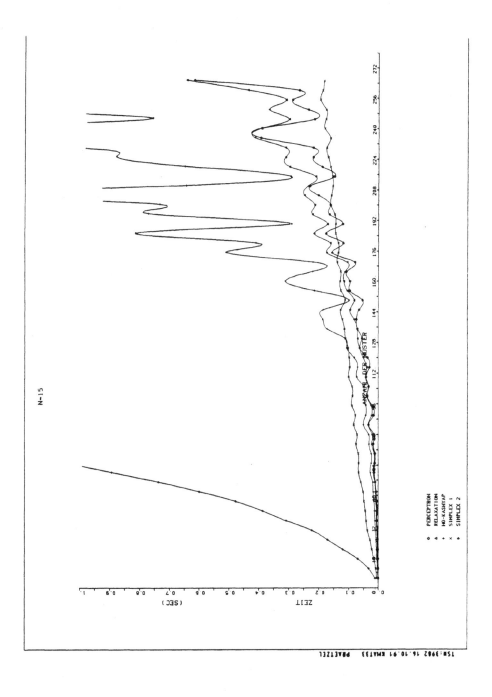

N=15

PERCEPTRON
RELAXATION
HO-KASHYAP
SIMPLEX 1
SIMPLEX 2

ANZAHL DER MUSTER

ZEIT (SEC)

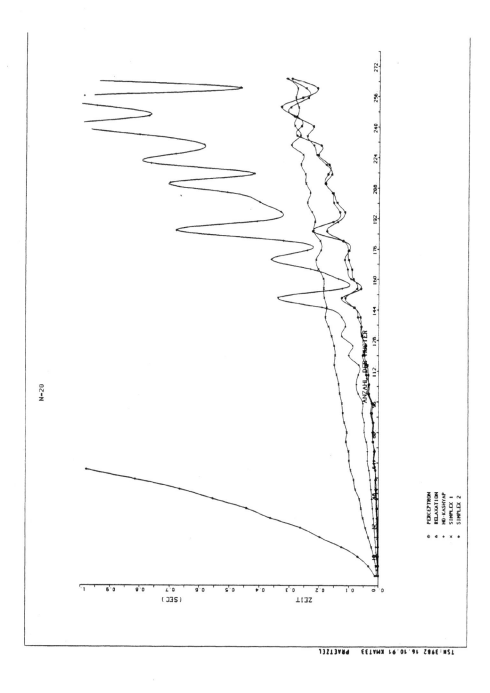

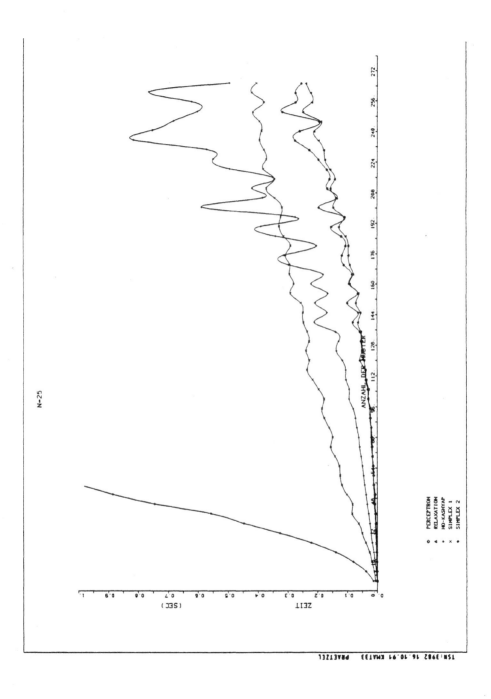

N-25

ANZAHL DER MUSTER

ZEIT (SEC)

PERCEPTRON
RELAXATION
HO-KASHYAP
SIMPLEX 1
SIMPLEX 2

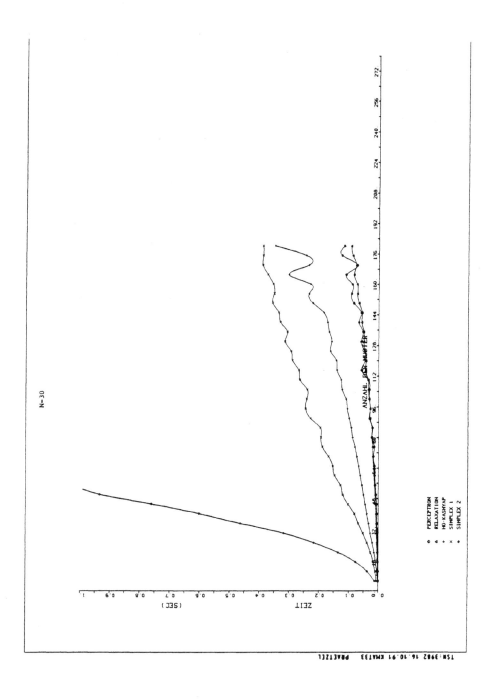

N-30

ANZAHL DER MUSTER

ZEIT (SEC)

PERCEPTRON
RELAXATION
HO-KASHYAP
SIMPLEX 1
SIMPLEX 2

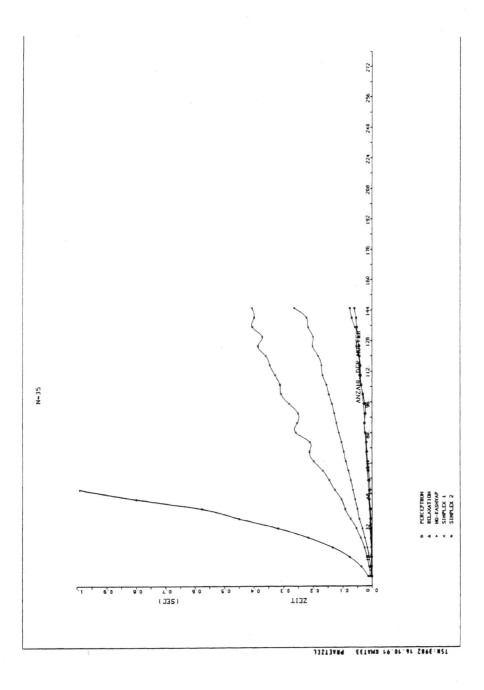

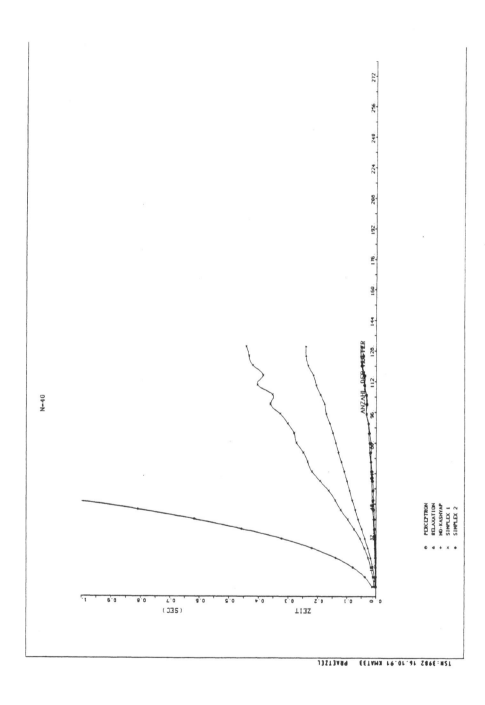

N-40

ZEIT (SEC)

ANZAHL DER MUSTER

- PERCEPTRON
- RELAXATION
- HO-KASHYAP
- SIMPLEX 1
- SIMPLEX 2

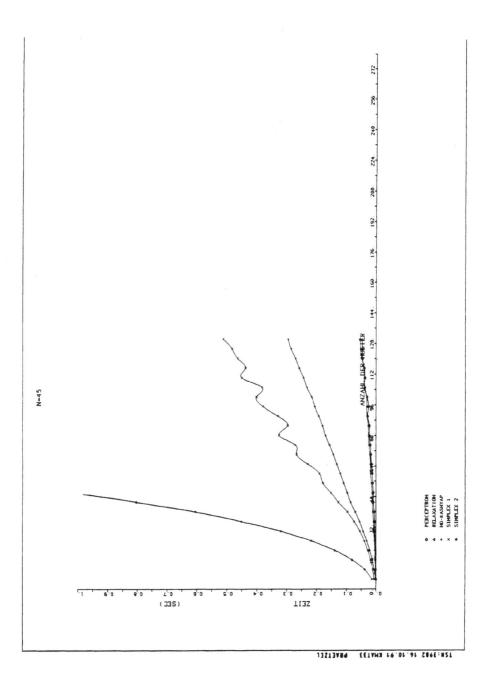

N=45

ANZAHL DER MUSTER

ZEIT (SEC)

◆ PERCEPTRON
▲ RELAXATION
+ HO-KASHYAP
× SIMPLEX 1
● SIMPLEX 2

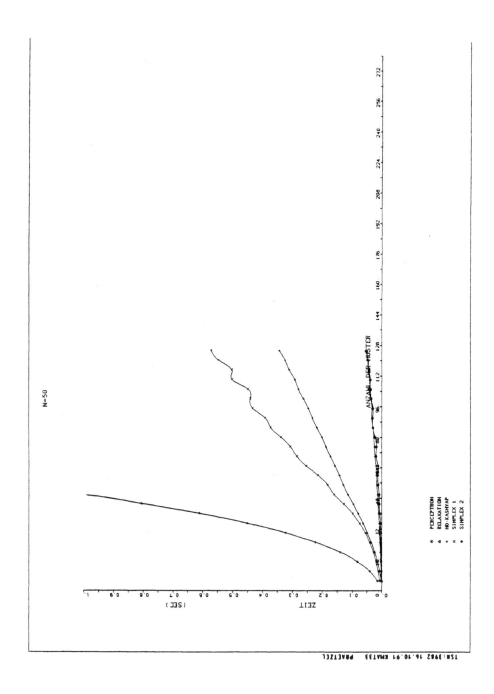

N=50

ANZAHL DER MUSTER

ZEIT (SEC)

PERCEPTRON
RELAXATION
HO-KASHYAP
SIMPLEX 1
SIMPLEX 2

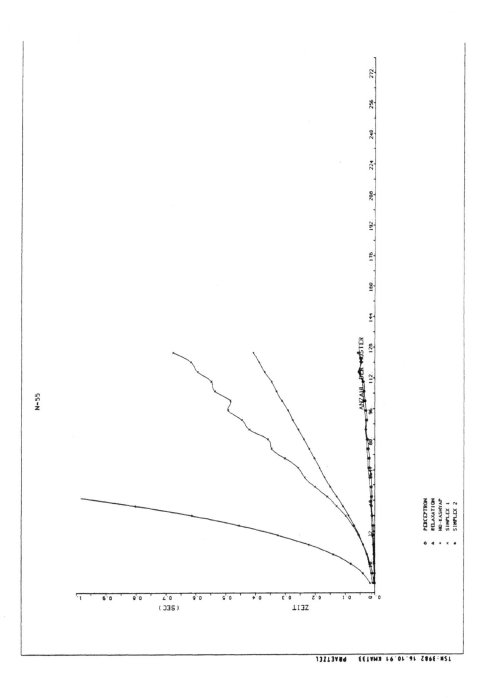

N-55

PERCEPTRON
RELAXATION
HO-KASHYAP
SIMPLEX 1
SIMPLEX 2

ANZAHL DER MUSTER

ZEIT (SEC)

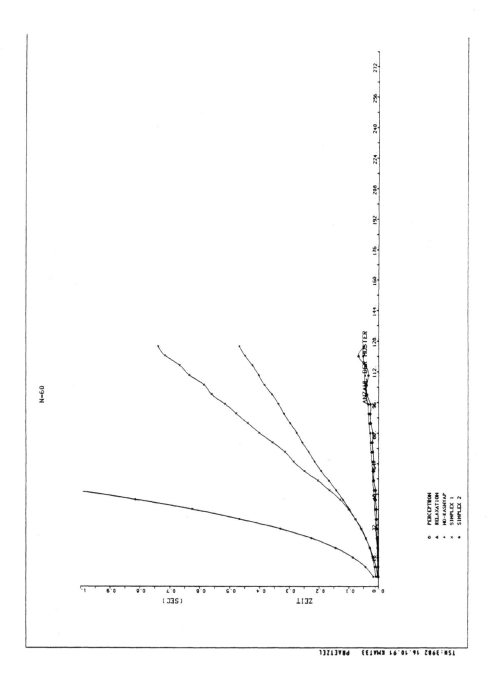

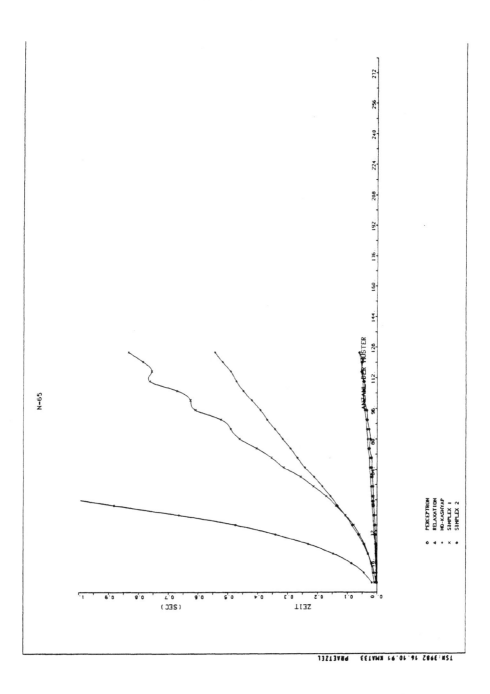

N–65

PERCEPTRON
RELAXATION
HO-KASHYAP
SIMPLEX 1
SIMPLEX 2

ANZAHL DER MUSTER

ZEIT
(SEC)

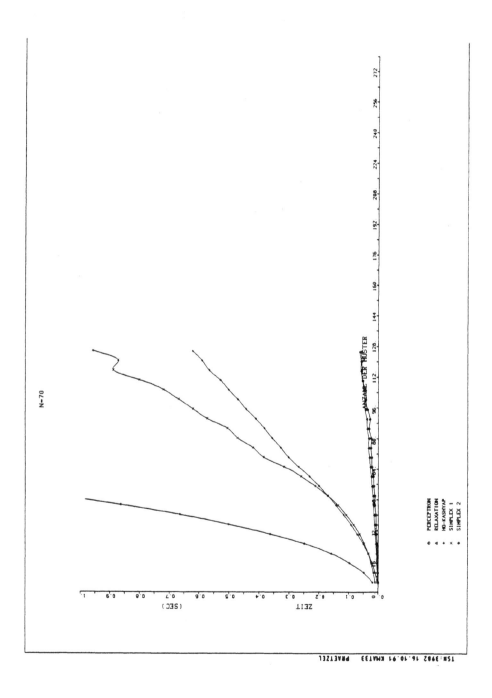

N-70

PERCEPTRON
RELAXATION
HO-KASHYAP
SIMPLEX 1
SIMPLEX 2

ANZAHL DER MUSTER

ZEIT (SEC)

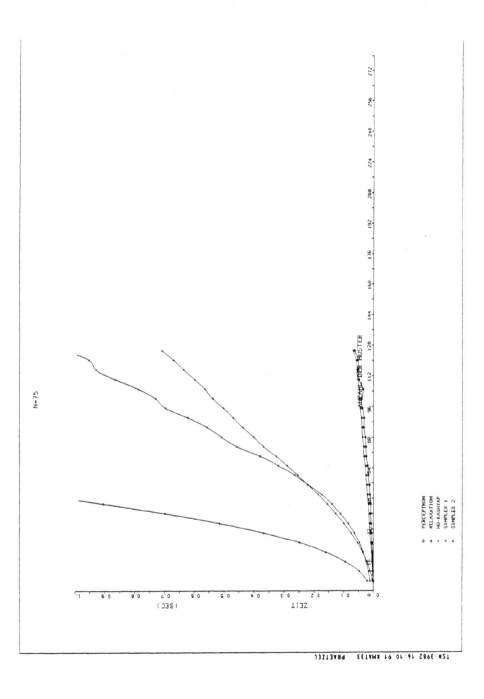

N-75

ANZAHL DER MUSTER

272 256 240 224 208 192 176 160 144 128 112 96 80 64 48

ZEIT (SEC)

1. 0.9 0.8 0.7 0.6 0.5 0.4 0.3 0.2 0.1 0 0

◇ PERCEPTRON
△ RELAXATION
+ HO-KASHYAP
× SIMPLEX 1
◆ SIMPLEX 2

www.ingramcontent.com/pod-product-compliance
Lightning Source LLC
LaVergne TN
LVHW052304060326
832902LV00021B/3695